Table of Contents

Dedication Page

Dedicated to El Gibor – Mighty God

Copyright Statement

Disclaimer

The book's content serves solely educational and informational objectives. The author and publisher have exerted maximum effort to present accurate information but do not take responsibility for any mistakes or results that stem from using this material. Professional advice should be obtained for specific OT cybersecurity situations by readers.

Permissions

For permissions requests, please contact: [Chukwudi Abalogu/Logusman] [Chukwudi.abalogu@gmail.com]

Prologue: The Invisible Battlefield

The background noise of power grids working alongside water pipelines carrying liquid and trains moving along tracks represent the hidden heartbeat of modern civilization which supports our global connectedness. The vital systems supporting our economies and societies remain hidden from everyday view while they sustain both the simple and complex aspects of daily life. At the heart of this critical infrastructure lies a network of sophisticated control systems: SCADA – Supervisory Control and Data Acquisition.

SCADA systems serve as silent protectors that oversee essential resource management including energy and water flows as well as transportation systems. SCADA systems function as the complex nerve centers of today's world by continuously gathering data and analyzing trends to execute necessary commands for the uninterrupted functioning of essential infrastructure. The dependable functioning of SCADA systems is essential because their breakdown causes multiple disruptions that can damage economies and pose public safety risks.

Although automated control systems are hidden from view they pose significant risks to users. The interconnected nature of SCADA systems enables operational efficiency while simultaneously creating security vulnerabilities. The digital revolution has created remarkable automation and control capabilities but simultaneously unveiled a new silent battlefield in the digital world which attacks critical systems essential to modern life.

Today's digital landscape represents an era defined by cyber threats as the boundaries between physical reality and digital existence continue to merge. Attackers motivated by financial benefit, political goals or pure evilness are now increasingly exploiting SCADA system vulnerabilities to interrupt operations, steal data and inflict physical damage. The consequences can be catastrophic: Cities face darkness from widespread power outages while contaminated water supplies endanger public health transportation networks stop working and industrial processes fall into disorder.

Such attacks typically manifest in covert ways that make detection very challenging. These attacks lack obvious physical destruction yet achieve their goal through stealthy infiltration followed by a progressive loss of operational control and systematic contamination. Gradual damage often proves more devastating because it unfolds slowly, which forces investigators to work hard to determine the root cause and restore fundamental services.

This book, Beyond the Firewall: Beyond the Firewall examines the hidden challenges faced when securing SCADA systems against modern cyber threats. The book examines SCADA system weaknesses and the advanced methods used by attackers along with the extensive defense mechanisms necessary to counter these threats. This urgent message encourages everyone from organizations to individuals to value SCADA security while adopting a proactive multi-layered defense strategy to protect essential modern infrastructure.

This discussion will focus on the technical details of SCADA systems including their structure, communication methods, and built-in weaknesses. Our exploration includes different cyber threats ranging from malware attacks to advanced persistent threats (APTs) while analyzing what drives these attacks. The study will focus on best practices for SCADA network protection alongside development of strong access controls and incident response strategies. Human factors stand as essential elements in security strategies which necessitate employee training development and the establishment of security awareness programs together with building a resilient security culture.

We will explore crucial regulatory compliance requirements and industry standards which are essential for strengthened security when followed properly. Our final discussion will focus on upcoming technologies and trends that will define SCADA security's future landscape.

This document functions as more than just a technical guide because it serves as an urgent call for action. The invisible battlefield exists while it involves very high consequences. Protecting our critical infrastructure requires more than technological expertise because it calls for everyone to unite in their commitment toward continuous vigilance and proactive measures to defend the systems essential to our contemporary existence. Together we must set out on this path as we investigate both the difficulties and possibilities presented by protecting the covert protectors of our linked world.

References:

Books:

Allen, P. (2017). Industrial cybersecurity: Protecting critical infrastructure.

https://20307279.fs1.hubspotusercontent-na1.net/hubfs/20307279/Documents%20and%20Downloads/Claroty-Industrial-Buyers-Guide.pdf?__hstc=125082197.02d2b99b55944b8bc7753837b20266e1.1740484446976.1740484446976.1740484446976.1&__hssc=125082197.1.1740484446976&__hsfp=965184237

Butterworth Heinemann Books - Internet of Things (IoT) - An Engineering Approach From Principles to Practice 1st Edition – (2024) Author: Xicai Yue

Slay, J., & Miller, M. (2007). Lessons learned from the maroochy water breach. https://dl.ifip.org/db/conf/ifip11-10/cip2007/SlayM07.pdf

Fortinet: Top 5 Critical Capabilities of a Detection and Response Platform

Andrew Davies, Mitchell Schneider, Rustam Malik, Eric Ahlm – Gartner Magic Quadrant for Security Information and Event Management (2024) https://www.fortinet.com/library/security-operations-solutionpfsid=Kaj7-bYmi1&_pfses=MQD3xb5NPowYNvnEk3rJkXs3

Alejandro Leal - Security Orchestration, Automation and Response (SOAR) (2024) https://www.kuppingercole.com/reprints/c07e2447200fc3ff935536b41591ff84

Cloud Range for Critical Infrastructure - https://www.cloudrangecyber.com/critical-infrastructure?utm_source=google&utm_medium=cpc&utm_campaign=ot&utm_term=critical%20infrastructure%20cybersecurity&utm_campaign=Operational+Technology&utm_source=adwords&utm_medium=ppc&hsa_acc=1978465621&hsa_cam=18471995404&hsa_grp=142064738077&hsa_ad=626199759758&hsa_src=g&hsa_tgt=kwd-11121400062&hsa_kw=critical%20infrastructure%20cybersecurity&hsa_mt=b&hsa_net=adwords&hsa_ver=3&gad_source=1&gclid=Cj0KCQiA8fW9BhC8ARIsACwHqYrmku3DyNY-lAnYd41jiZdqfYr9EmDcEmzd1M8M7wl3jAb7jqjGYXoaAl-LEALw_wcB

senhasegura-ebook-shielding-critical-infrastructure.pdf

Langner, R. (2011). Stuxnet: Dissecting a cyberwarfare weapon. IEEE Security & Privacy, 9(3), 49-51.

Journal Articles: Falliere, N., O. Murchu, and E. Chien. (2011). “W32. Stuxnet Dossier.” Symantec Security Response.

Langner, R. (2013). Stuxnet: Dissecting a cyberwarfare weapon. IEEE Security & Privacy, 11(3), 49–51.

Lee, R. M., Langley, R., & Jeong, H. (2011). A survey of SCADA security systems. International Journal of Critical Infrastructure Protection, 4(3), 101–114.

Conference Papers:

R. Khan et al., "Energy Sustainability–Survey on Technology and Control of Microgrid, Smart Grid and Virtual Power Plant," in IEEE Access, vol. 9, pp. 104663-104694, 2021, doi: 10.1109/ACCESS.2021.3099941.

keywords: {Microgrids; Smart grids; Renewable energy sources; Europe; Sustainable development; Power system stability; Australia; Climate change; Controllers; cyber security; microgrid;

renewable energy; smart grid; system architectures; virtual power plant; world market},

B. Babu, T. Ijyas, Muneer P. and J. Varghese, "Security issues in SCADA based industrial control systems," 2017 2nd International Conference on Anti-Cyber Crimes (ICACC), Abha, Saudi Arabia, 2017, pp. 47-51, doi: 10.1109/Anti-Cybercrime.2017.7905261. keywords: {Integrated circuits; SCADA systems; Protocols; Authentication; Process control; Industrial Control; Cyber-attacks; SCADA},

Arastoo Zibaeirad, Farnoosh Koleini, Shengping Bi, Tao Hou, Tao Wang. "A Comprehensive Survey on the Security of Smart Grid: Challenges, Mitigations, and Future Research Opportunities" https://arxiv.org/abs/2407.07966

Abdellah Chehri,*ORCID,Issouf Fofana ORCID and Xiaomin Yang. (2021) Security Risk Modeling in Smart Grid Critical Infrastructures in the Era of Big Data and Artificial Intelligence

Sean Weerakkody, Omur Ozel, Yilin Mo and Bruno Sinopoli (2019), "Resilient Control in Cyber-Physical Systems: Countering Uncertainty, Constraints, and Adversarial Behavior", Foundations and Trends® in Systems and Control: Vol. 7: No. 1-2, pp 1-252. http://dx.doi.org/10.1561/2600000018

Government Reports and White Papers:

United States Department of Homeland Security. (2023). National Cybersecurity Strategy. Washington, DC: DHS.

National Institute of Standards and Technology (NIST). (2015). NIST Cybersecurity Framework. Gaithersburg, MD: NIST.

Industrial Control Systems Cyber Emergency Response Team (ICS-CERT). (Various years). Alerts and Advisories. [https://dione.lib.unipi.gr/xmlui/handle/unipi/16553]

Standards and Regulations:

North American Electric Reliability Corporation (NERC). (2012, 2020). NERC Critical Infrastructure Protection (CIP) Standards. [T. Tibbals and D. Dolezilek, "Communications Technologies and Practices to Satisfy NERC Critical Infrastructure Protection (CIP)," 2006 Power Systems Conference: Advanced Metering, Protection, Control, Communication, and Distributed Resources, Clemson, SC, USA, 2006, pp. 454-479, doi: 10.1109/PSAMP.2006.285415. keywords: {Communications technology; Protection; Computer security; ISO standards; Standards organizations; IEC standards; ANSI standards; Standards development; Councils; Information security},].

International Organization for Standardization (ISO). (2013). ISO/IEC 27001:2013 Information security management systems—Requirements. Geneva: ISO.

Chapter 1: Introduction to SCADA Systems and Their Importance

The global interconnected landscape now requires technology as an essential foundation for every industrial sector more than at any previous time. SCADA systems control critical infrastructure networks while separate systems facilitate daily life operations. SCADA systems execute essential service functions through the management of urban power supply grids and municipal water purification systems. As digital systems undergo modernization through integration processes, they expose new vulnerabilities to cyber threats.

Understanding SCADA Systems

Industrial control systems known as SCADA systems monitor and control physical process operations. The architecture of SCADA systems develops through the integration of its multiple components to function as a cohesive unit.

Remote Terminal Units (RTUs): Remote Terminal Units function as field devices which collect sensor data and send it to the central SCADA system. RTUs oversee industrial process operations by following instructions received from the SCADA system.

Programmable Logic Controllers (PLCs): PLCs handle automation tasks that RTUs perform but offer improved flexibility together with superior logic processing abilities.

Human-Machine Interface (HMI): Operators access and control systems through the Human-Machine Interface which serves as the main SCADA interaction point. While managing process alerts and tasks the system displays graphical data visualizations.

Communication Infrastructure: The communication protocols enable network components to create connections between RTUs PLCs HMIs for data transmission support.

Central Server: The primary SCADA system operates through the central server which handles data processing and historical record storage while granting users data analysis capabilities.

SCADA systems operate within real-time environments which allows operators to track system performance continuously. SCADA systems enable rapid decision-making through data analysis which enhances both operational efficiency and safety standards.

The Critical Role of SCADA in Infrastructure

SCADA systems function as core components across numerous operational environments. SCADA systems function as vital operational tools across multiple industrial sectors.

Utilities: SCADA systems preserve power grid stability through effective electricity generation control and balanced electrical load distribution. SCADA systems utilize fast analysis to avoid power outages and optimize energy demand management.

Water and Wastewater Management: SCADA systems oversee the operations of drinking water distribution networks and wastewater treatment facilities. SCADA systems operate to ensure water quality standards are met and manage reservoir levels according to environmental regulatory requirements.

Transportation: SCADA systems enable traffic management for transportation systems by supporting railroad operations and airport functions. SCADA systems use vehicle tracking to improve traffic navigation while also maintaining passenger safety.

Manufacturing: SCADA systems enable manufacturing operations by automating production processes and monitoring production lines. Implementation of this strategy produces higher production efficiency, enhanced product standards and reduced downtime intervals.

SCADA systems gain increased importance because they create linkages between different industrial sectors. Network disruptions become extensive when SCADA systems fail, which shows the need for strong security measures together with dependable performance.

The Evolving Threat Landscape

The development of SCADA systems has created environments that face increased security threats. Traditional SCADA systems achieved reduced security risk exposure by functioning within isolated operational settings. The integration of IoT technology with remote access capabilities and enhanced connectivity has fundamentally transformed operational environments. Technological improvements which enhanced operational efficiency also opened significant cybersecurity vulnerabilities.

SCADA systems environments must defend against multiple types of cyber threats that utilize varying attack methods.

Malware Attacks: SCADA systems face operational disruption and data theft risks from malware attacks. The Stuxnet cyber-attack against Iranian nuclear facilities revealed severe weaknesses in key infrastructure systems.

Phishing and Social Engineering: Human error remains a significant vulnerability. SCADA systems become vulnerable to security threats when employees fall victim to phishing attacks that lead them to share credentials or install harmful software.

Denial of Service (DoS) Attacks: SCADA systems become nonfunctional due to excessive traffic from attackers which leads to disruptions in essential services.

Insider Threats: Disloyal staff members together with external contractors who have system access use their permissions to take control of system operations and steal data.

Organizations need to develop sophisticated security strategies that go past basic perimeter defenses such as firewalls to handle new cybersecurity threats. To achieve complete security protection SCADA systems, require integrated technical controls human factors and operational procedures.

The Importance of Cybersecurity in SCADA Systems

SCADA systems serve as the fundamental infrastructure framework and any cybersecurity breach against them leads to severe consequences. Cyberattacks that succeed both disrupt operations and breach data which subsequently result in regulatory fines.

Operational Disruption: Breaches that shut down essential services lead to financial losses for organizations and produce safety risks while tarnishing their reputations.

Data Breaches: Business operations become vulnerable when unauthorized parties access sensitive information which facilitates intellectual property theft and customer data breaches.

Regulatory Consequences: Various industries must adhere to rigorous regulations to preserve their operational systems and protect sensitive information. Organizations experience substantial financial damage and face legal penalties when data breaches occur alongside damaged trust relationships with stakeholders and the public.

Safety Risks: Cybersecurity attacks create immediate safety threats within the energy and transportation sectors. Hacks of transportation systems disrupt operations and endanger passengers while SCADA system attacks lead to unpredictable power grid outages.

The Need for Enhanced Security Measures

SCADA systems-dependent organizations need robust security protocols to operate safely in the face of changing threat landscapes. Organizations need to develop security measures which integrate technical solutions with an organizational culture dedicated to security. Key strategies include:

Risk Assessment and Management: Organizations can detect and address potential vulnerabilities by conducting frequent SCADA system risk assessments. Organizations need to evaluate threats and create risk management plans to safeguard important resources.

Incident Response Planning: Organizations need to establish well-defined incident response plans to minimize the damage from cyber incidents. The strategy needs to detail team member responsibilities and define communication protocols and recovery procedures.

Employee Training and Awareness: Cybersecurity practices depend fundamentally on human elements. Employees maintain their cybersecurity capabilities through ongoing training programs which teach them to recognize phishing attacks, master password security and build proactive threat detection skills.

Continuous Monitoring: Real-time detection of security anomalies and intrusions becomes possible through continuous monitoring solutions. Organizations deploy SIEM systems to analyze network activity because these systems deliver crucial insights that enable rapid incident responses.

Network Segmentation: Organizations use network segmentation to protect their systems by both restricting attacker movement and containing security breaches. SCADA security system gets strengthened because this process separates different system components to prevent unauthorized access between them.

The Role of Industry Standards and Compliance

To ensure SCADA system security organizations must follow industry standards and meet regulatory requirements. Organizations obtain cybersecurity risk management guidance through the application of the National Institute of Standards and Technology Cybersecurity Framework and ISO 27001 from the International Organization for Standardization. Organizations achieve system protection and energy sector compliance by following NERC CIP regulations.

Conclusion: The Path Forward

The book demonstrates SCADA system vulnerabilities are multifaceted in nature and shows protection requires diverse strategies beyond technical measures because these challenges exist across various dimensions. Organizations must carry out constant system evaluations and continuous improvements to effectively tackle new and emerging threats.

The upcoming sections evaluate SCADA security through an analysis of risk management procedures and incident response frameworks while focusing on workforce education together with technology enhancements. This material presents fundamental knowledge and tools for organizations to strengthen SCADA security allowing them to shield critical infrastructure systems from cyber risks while maintaining dependable system performance and safety.

Organizations maintain effective essential societal service security by investing in cybersecurity alongside developing security culture and implementing threat awareness protection strategies. By uniting our resources, we advanced-past standard firewall protection to develop advanced security solutions for both SCADA systems and their critical infrastructure networks.

The Complex Interdependencies of SCADA Systems

To grasp the full significance of SCADA systems it is essential to understand their intricate links to critical infrastructure components. SCADA systems function through the combination of various technologies and services within an operational network. For example:

Integration with IoT Devices: SCADA systems gather useful data from multiple advanced devices that feature IoT technology design. Real-time monitoring solutions emerge from smart sensors which deliver environmental data together with equipment performance information and operational metrics. Monitoring and control systems' capability expansion creates new access points which attackers target and these areas require urgent protection.

Communication Protocols: SCADA system operations require essential communication protocols such as Modbus, DNP3, and OPC. To ensure operational effectiveness and strong security measures organizations need to deeply understand communication protocols. Modbus maintains its vulnerability to protocol threats due to its absence of basic security measures to prevent unauthorized access and packet interception. To ensure their communication networks remain secure, organizations need to pinpoint protocol vulnerabilities.

Supply Chain Dependencies: SCADA systems primarily source their hardware and software components from third-party vendors. Vendor system breaches through supply chain dependencies result in SCADA security becoming compromised. For risk reduction organizations must evaluate vendor security protocols thoroughly and develop strong cybersecurity agreements.

The Human Element: Addressing the Weakest Link

Advanced technology powers SCADA systems yet human vulnerabilities present the main security threat. When employees and their external partners fail to maintain adequate vigilance or awareness, they inadvertently create security risks.

Creating a Security Awareness Culture: Organizations must build a security-focused workplace culture that educates every employee about SCADA system protection measures. Through regular training sessions combined with informative newsletters that provide interactive workshops employees learn cybersecurity techniques to maintain their cybersecurity awareness. The workforce needs to trust that they can report unusual activities in a safe environment without fearing retribution.

Access Control and Privilege Management: Organizations need to establish strict access management protocols to protect SCADA systems effectively. The least privilege principle provides foundational guidelines for defining user roles and permissions. Organizations can reduce insider threats by giving employees access only to necessary systems and information required for their job roles.

Incident Reporting Mechanisms: Organizations can create defined reporting channels which ensure quick responses to security threats. Staff training programs equip employees with the skills needed to detect suspicious behavior while instructing them in proper procedures for reporting phishing emails and system anomalies.

The Future of SCADA Security

The cybersecurity landscape demands ongoing modifications for SCADA systems because of the continuous progression of technology. Several emerging trends are worth noting:

Artificial Intelligence and Machine Learning: Artificial intelligence and machine learning boost cybersecurity effectiveness by advancing threat detection abilities and response strategies. Organizations can analyze massive data volumes to identify potential cyber threat patterns and enhance their response times through preventative strategies with these technologies.

Blockchain Technology: SCADA security professionals now see blockchain technology as essential because its significance continues to increase. SCADA systems benefit from blockchain technology because its immutable ledger framework maintains data integrity and authenticates data. Blockchain technology requires data provenance in specific settings to demonstrate its unique benefits.

Zero Trust Architecture: According to Zero Trust principles organizations need to treat everyone inside and outside their networks with suspicion until their identities are verified. Modern SCADA security systems control access by ensuring every user and system device must authenticate their identity continuously. Organizations witness significant reductions in unauthorized access risks by implementing Zero Trust principles.

Collaboration and Information Sharing: Within the cybersecurity community there is a shared belief that collaborative efforts among organizations generate strong solutions to their common security threats. Organizations gain advantages from the exchange of threat intelligence and best practices through their respective industry information-sharing groups via ICS-CERT.

Conclusion: The Call to Action

"Beyond the Firewall" marks the beginning of our study of SCADA security by showing how critical SCADA systems function operationally. SCADA systems present significant threats to public safety and national security that extend beyond mere technical challenges.

This publication examines cutting-edge approaches and technologies together with established best practices for enhancing SCADA system security. Organizations enhance their cybersecurity defenses by understanding risks thoroughly and applying forward-thinking protective strategies.

The improvement of SCADA security system requires joint efforts from management teams, technical teams and frontline employees. Our goal is to develop a strong protection system that defends essential infrastructure and builds public trust in fundamental systems.

The following chapters examine comprehensive risk assessment planning strategies along with incident response techniques and advanced technology applications while also covering employee education initiatives. This publication serves as a guidebook that helps readers understand vital SCADA system protection information while teaching practical protection strategies.

The Imperative of Proactive Security

The security of SCADA systems requires organizations to implement proactive cybersecurity measures to remain effective. Traditional IT security measures respond after incidents happen which necessitate SCADA systems to adopt security strategies that function before incidents happen. Preventative measures need to be established by organizations through early identification of potential threats to block security breaches. Here's why a proactive stance is essential:

Dynamic Threat Landscape: Cyber threats grow more complex and evolve faster with technological advancements. Attackers utilize advanced technologies such as machine learning and automated systems to discover and exploit weaknesses in systems. Organizations preserve their security advantage by continuously analyzing threats and updating security protocols to address emerging risks.

Cost-Effectiveness: Businesses avoid expensive recovery costs and protect their reputation through early detection and correction of system vulnerability. Businesses that implement proactive cybersecurity measures before cyberattacks occur generate better financial outcomes.

Regulatory Compliance: Several sectors operate under stringent cybersecurity regulations. Organizations follow regulatory guidelines and get ready for audits through proactive strategies that also ensure industry compliance.

Building Trust and Reliability: Maintaining public trust should be a top priority for organizations operating critical infrastructure systems. Robust cybersecurity measures in organizations demonstrate dependability to customers and stakeholders which strengthens their reputation.

Moving Forward: Key Concepts to Explore

The book offers readers essential concepts and actionable frameworks which enhance SCADA system security. Some key topics will include:

Risk Management Frameworks: This section illustrates the practical implementation of recognized security frameworks such as NIST and ISO 27001 in SCADA system protection. Through risk assessment procedures and asset identification readers can discern the security controls that require immediate attention.

Incident Response and Recovery Protocols: Organizations can minimize potential damage effectively when they possess knowledge of cyber incident response protocols. Our detailed incident response plans guide organizations through quick detection of incidents and ensure fast recovery by managing responses with efficiency.

Emerging Technologies and Security Innovations: The publication examines sophisticated technologies that enhance SCADA security using AI analytics and encryption improvements along with modern communication protocol standards. Organizations can defend themselves against new security threats by implementing these cutting-edge tools.

Real-World Case Studies: The publication examines confirmed SCADA security incidents and offers useful protection methods. Real-world case studies showcase essential security practices as they reveal vulnerabilities caused by inadequate protection systems.

Conclusion: Collective Responsibility

Organizational members across all departments need to collaborate in SCADA system protection since IT and cybersecurity specialists alone are incapable of managing it. Both executive leaders and operational staff members should understand their respective security obligations. Cybersecurity demands ongoing vigilance and flexibility from organizations because it requires perpetual work that is never fully finished.

As we embark on this journey through "Beyond the Firewall: The partnership in "Beyond the Firewall: Enhancing SCADA Security in the Age of Cyber Threats" requires active defense strategies to protect critical infrastructure from emerging cyber threats. Organizations that focus their cultural development on security while actively investing resources and updating their knowledge about new threats and technologies create dependable systems that protect their institutions as well as the communities and economies that rely on them.

This first chapter introduces readers to SCADA system intricacies and security issues while emphasizing cybersecurity's crucial role. The subsequent chapters offer actionable methods and valuable insights to enhance SCADA system protection from active digital dangers. By working together, we establish robust protection for essential infrastructure systems that go beyond standard compliance requirements.

Chapter 2: Understanding the Cyber Threat Landscape

The cybersecurity challenges found in SCADA systems demonstrate why understanding cyber threat dynamics is essential for developing effective security approaches. The analysis of cyber threats against SCADA systems is presented in this chapter alongside discussions of attacker motives and organizational impacts on critical infrastructure operations. This analysis of authentic case studies demonstrates the probable results of cyber threats while providing strategies for organizations to prepare and respond effectively.

The Nature of Cyber Threats

Cyber threats classification requires analyzing attacker goals along with the chosen attack methodologies and the complexity levels of threats. Organizations can establish effective protection against cyber-attacks by understanding diverse threat categories.

1. Malware Attacks

The term 'Malware' refers to harmful software which seeks to disrupt computer operations through damage to system parts and unauthorized system access. SCADA systems face numerous malware types that pursue distinct goals and execute a range of attack methods.

Viruses: Viruses function as self-replicating software which binds to legitimate programs to propagate across systems while they threaten file integrity and system stability.

Worms: Worms propagate themselves through network connections without assistance by utilizing software vulnerabilities for their distribution.

Trojan Horses: Trojan Horse programs conceal their malicious functionalities by disguising themselves as legitimate software to deceive users into downloading them. Hacker programs gain activation which enables them to access systems without authorization.

Ransomware: Ransomware stands apart from other malware types because it uses encryption to lock victim files then requires payment for access restoration. Attacks on critical infrastructure cause major operational disruptions and put public safety at risk.

The Stuxnet worm became infamous for being malware because it attacked Iran's nuclear facilities through SCADA systems. Security experts agree that nation-state hackers created Stuxnet to sabotage the PLCs that operate nuclear centrifuges. The incident demonstrated malware's ability to physically damage essential infrastructure networks.

2. Phishing and Social Engineering Attacks

Phishing attacks deceive individuals into sharing sensitive information by disguising malicious requests as trustworthy entities. Cyber attackers trick people into clicking dangerous links by sending fake emails that look real.

Social engineering attacks combine impersonation with deceptive manipulation strategies to take advantage of human mental vulnerabilities. Attackers often access SCADA systems or confidential information by impersonating coworkers, IT staff members, and vendor representatives.

Phishing emails designed to look like system update notifications lure employees into providing their login details on fraudulent websites. When an attacker infiltrates a SCADA system it causes major operational disruptions.

3. DoS attacks create heavy traffic to disable systems while DDoS attacks deploy several compromised machines to create flood traffic that prevents legitimate users from gaining access.

Denial of Service attacks overload systems or networks with excessive traffic to block access. During Distributed Denial of Service attacks attackers utilized numerous infected machines within a botnet which delivers massive traffic loads to the targeted system thereby preventing legitimate user access.

SCADA systems experience significant operational disruptions when they are subjected to DoS or DDoS attacks. Operators may lose access to essential data needed for water quality control during a distributed denial of service attack on water treatment facility monitoring systems.

4. Insider Threats

Employees and contractors who abuse their SCADA system access become insider threats to organizations. Organizations encounter security challenges that arise from malicious insiders intentionally misusing their access rights and employees who unintentionally generate vulnerabilities through careless actions.

A serious incident happened when a chemical facility employee manipulated SCADA system settings to create hazardous operating conditions. To effectively handle internal security threats organizations must implement robust access controls and monitoring systems.

5. Advanced Persistent Threats (APTs)

Advanced Persistent Threats (APTs) are complex cyber-attacks that focus on organizations and engage in long-term operations. Cyber attackers use multiple techniques to obtain unauthorized access to networks which they keep open for long durations to steal sensitive information or disrupt critical services.

Advanced Persistent Threats (APTs) focus on energy, water, and manufacturing sectors because they heavily rely on SCADA systems. Cybercriminals infiltrate networks through social engineering tactics paired with malware deployment and reconnaissance techniques and maintain their stealth to collect intelligence while preparing further malicious activities.

The Dragonfly campaign illustrates an APT attack when it targeted SCADA systems at energy facilities across both the United States and Europe. SCADA network access was achieved by attackers who used spear-phishing techniques alongside vulnerabilities in third-party software to collect operational system data.

Motivations Behind Cyber Attacks on SCADA Systems

Organizations need insights into attacker motives to develop effective security strategies for SCADA systems. Attackers may pursue various objectives, including:

1. Financial Gain

Cybercriminals initiate attacks with the expectation of receiving financial benefits through their activities. This can be manifested in several ways:

Ransomware Attacks: Ransomware attacks operate by encrypting critical data and then demand payment for decryption keys. SCADA system-dependent organizations become prime targets for cyber extortionists because they must pay ransoms to get their operations back online quickly.

Data Theft: The primary objective for hackers stealing sensitive information like intellectual property and trade secrets is to sell them on dark web platforms or deploy them against competing companies.

Fraud: Attackers exploiting SCADA system vulnerabilities modify financial transactions to reroute funds thereby causing financial damage to organizations.

2. Political or Ideological Motives

Politically motivated hacker groups and government-backed operators target SCADA systems to advance their political objectives and ideological convictions. These threats can take various forms:

Cyber Warfare: Nation-states implement cyber warfare tactics to disable their adversaries' essential infrastructure systems. Stuxnet malware stands as a primary illustration of cyber operations with political aims devised to block Iran's nuclear development.

Hacktivism: Hacktivist groups like Anonymous launch attacks against institutions including government bodies and environmental polluters which they identify as their adversaries. The main goal of attackers is to interrupt existing systems while revealing supposed wrongdoing.

3. Espionage

Industrial espionage represents one of the primary security threats for businesses operating in competitive markets. Malicious actors target SCADA systems to learn about industrial operations and technological developments. These attacks use APT methods that allow them to stay hidden while they collect sensitive data over long timeframes.

Companies compete by targeting an energy firm to obtain information about advanced technologies and operational efficiencies which they believe will give them a competitive advantage.

4. Revenge or Disgruntlement

Employees who hold personal grievances against organizations frequently become insider threats by taking damaging actions. Disgruntled employees who know the SCADA system can utilize their expertise to both damage operations and steal data while generating hazardous situations. Recent events show organizations must build supportive work environments and implement monitoring systems to detect employee dissatisfaction.

Actual Cyber Threats to SCADA Systems include several documented real-world incidents.

Real-world cyber-attack data analysis uncovers critical insights about SCADA system risks while demonstrating how insufficient security measures can trigger major impacts.

1. In 2015 a complex cyber-attack affected Ukrainian power grid systems and caused blackouts for 230,000 residents.

In December 2015 Ukrainian power grids faced a complex cyber-attack that caused blackouts for 230,000 people. State-sponsored Russian hackers supposedly took over SCADA systems responsible for power infrastructure operations to execute a coordinated attack against substations.

Attackers deployed malware featuring the Black Energy Trojan as employees received spear-phishing emails during the incident. The operations faced major disruptions because attackers manipulated the systems. This event demonstrates how critical infrastructure faces severe threats from cyber-attacks while making it clear that strong cybersecurity defenses are essential.

2. A petrochemical facility became the target of a cyber-attack involving Triton malware which compromised its safety systems in 2017.

Saudi Arabian petrochemical facility safety systems faced a cyber-attack from Triton malware in 2017. A cyber threat deployed Triton malware to attack the Triconex safety instrumented system (SIS) which could lead to disastrous results.

The planned attack did not cause physical damage because security teams detected it before any harm occurred. The event demonstrated the vulnerability of critical systems that attackers can exploit to interfere with both operational safety controls and fundamental safety standards. The event demonstrated the necessity of securing SCADA systems and safety protocols against cyber-attacks.

3. The Colonial Pipeline Ransomware Attack (2021)

The Colonial Pipeline serving almost half of East Coast fuel needs suffered a ransomware attack in May 2021. A Darkside cybercrime group executed an attack on Colonial Pipeline's network which allowed them to encrypt essential data and force the company to stop operations temporarily.

This ransomware attack triggered extensive fuel supply disruptions and highlighted how critical infrastructure systems face vulnerability to cyber threats. The cyber-attack forced Colonial Pipeline to pay hackers a ransom of $4.4 million. The attack shows organizational need for robust security measures and comprehensive response plans to mitigate ransomware threat effects.

Implications of Cyber Threats on SCADA Systems

Cyber threats directed at SCADA systems have far-reaching consequences that endanger public safety and undermine both economic stability and national security.

1. Operational Disruption

Cybersecurity breaches of SCADA systems lead to major disruptions in operational activities. This can be manifested in various ways, including:

Service Interruptions: Successful cyber-attacks force organizations to halt their critical operations as they address the resulting security breach. The need to halt water processing emerges when cyber attackers infiltrate a water treatment facility's SCADA system to prevent contamination from reaching consumers and to mitigate public health risks along with economic losses.

Production Delays: Cyber-attacks cause production line stoppages in the manufacturing sector resulting in supply chain delays and delayed product delivery. Companies that require timely deliveries experience cascading problems from disruptions which subsequently result in decreased customer satisfaction and financial loss.

2. Safety Risks

Cyber threats create dangers to public safety which extend past operational disruptions. SCADA systems control essential infrastructure that directly affects public health and safety through their management of critical processes.

Power Generation and Distribution: Cyber-attacks on power grids result in uncontrolled outages which interfere with critical services like hospitals emergency services and transportation systems. Blackouts result in severe consequences for densely populated areas where citizens require continuous electrical power.

Chemical and Environmental Hazards: SCADA systems at hazardous material facilities could face devastating effects if security breaches occur. A cyber-attack on safety controls at a chemical plant can cause hazardous spills and explosions while releasing toxic emissions which would endanger both plant workers and nearby residents.

3. Financial Losses

Organizations face substantial financial burdens as a result of cyber threats. Organizations may face:

Direct Costs: Remediation expenses include payments for cybersecurity professionals and costs for system repairs and equipment replacements. The Colonial Pipeline ransom payment during the outage was a small portion of the total expenditure which included costs for recovery activities and reputational damage to the company.

Indirect Costs: The financial consequences of cybersecurity incidents extend beyond direct remediation costs by causing operational downtime that results in lost revenue through diminished productivity and disrupted supply chains. A decrease in customer trust leads to reduced sales which creates prolonged financial problems for businesses.

Regulatory Fines: Companies that break cybersecurity rules risk facing substantial monetary fines and legal action. Companies that disregard data protection alongside secure operational environments face regulatory audits resulting in extra financial requirements.

4. Reputational Damage

A cyber event can produce severe damage to the reputation of an organization. Maintaining public perception is essential for organizations that operate critical infrastructure to succeed. Following a successful attack organization may experience:

Loss of Trust: Customers and stakeholders together with the public might start questioning an organization's ability to protect sensitive information while guaranteeing service continuity. Organizations face enormous difficulties in regaining trust once lost because reliability is fundamental to their field.

Negative Media Attention: Media coverage of high-profile cyber incidents amplifies negative public opinion toward the organizations that are impacted. Media attention following security breaches creates additional damage to organizations' reputations while simultaneously eroding public trust over time.

Preparing for Cyber Threats: A Proactive Approach

SCADA systems face increasing threats which require organizations to implement proactive cybersecurity measures. A comprehensive strategy demands risk assessment and employee training while it develops incident response plans and establishes ongoing monitoring measures.

1. Risk Assessment and Management

Routine risk assessments are essential to identify weaknesses in SCADA systems. Organizations should evaluate:

Asset Inventory: Organizations need to perform an inventory of essential assets within their SCADA systems including hardware components, software applications and data repositories. The first step to creating effective security strategies starts with identifying protection needs.

Threat Analysis: The organization needs to analyze possible threats within its unique environment to discover potential risks. Security evaluations must include examinations of diverse attack methods including internal security risks and malware threats as well as attacks from external sources.

Impact Evaluation: Examine the potential effects multiple cyber threats could have on an organization's operational functionality. Security teams can prioritize their protective measures based on potential impact assessments of cybersecurity threats.

2. Employee Training and Awareness

Employees serve as the chief defense mechanism against cybersecurity risks. Extensive training programs must be established by organizations to tackle cyber threats.

Phishing Awareness: Organizations witness reduced cyber-attack incidents after employees receive training to recognize phishing and suspicious email threats.

Safe Practices: Organizations strengthen their security measures by teaching employees to use strong passwords and activate multi-factor authentication together with instructions to report suspicious activity.

Incident Reporting: When employees adhere to established security incident reporting protocols, they maintain heightened alertness and take proactive steps against potential threats.

3. Incident Response Planning

Effective incident response plans are essential for minimizing the impact of cyber incidents. Organizations should develop:

Response Teams: Organizations must establish incident response teams where each member has clearly defined roles and responsibilities. Specialized training must be provided for these teams to enable them to handle various types of incidents effectively.

Communication Protocols: Establish communication procedures that will guide interactions with internal and external stakeholders during an incident. Effective communication allows organizations to maintain control over situations and ensure stakeholders remain fully updated.

Post-Incident Reviews: Organizations build better incident response skills through post-incident reviews that reveal improvement areas and direct updates to their response procedures.

Testing and Drills: Organizations must regularly perform incident response plan tests through tabletop exercises and simulations. When team members participate in these drills, they learn their responsibilities and build their ability to respond effectively in real emergency situations. When teams simulate ransomware attacks, they develop skills to handle complex real-world scenarios involving law enforcement and media interactions.

Documentation and Reporting: The need to keep thorough records for all incidents and resolutions continues to be vital for future analysis. Maintaining documentation enables organizations to meet compliance standards and identify patterns of attacks which allows them to strengthen their security measures over time.

4. Continuous Monitoring and Threat Intelligence

Regular monitoring of SCADA systems enables organizations to identify potential threats early on. This involves:

Real-Time Surveillance: Security information and event management (SIEM) systems allow organizations to monitor network traffic and user actions and system logs in real time. This system allows organizations to identify irregular patterns that indicate potential security breaches.

Threat Intelligence Sharing: By participating in information-sharing programs industries obtain enhanced situational awareness and receive crucial information about imminent threats. Collaboration between companies and cybersecurity groups allows for mutual exchange of threat intelligence data and successful practices.

Anomaly Detection Systems: Through the combination of machine learning algorithms with advanced analytics organizations can identify abnormal behavior in SCADA networks which allows them to establish preemptive measures against escalating breaches.

5. Implementing Security Controls and Best Practices

Organizations must implement robust security controls to protect SCADA systems from potential attacks. These controls should include:

Network Segmentation: Dividing the SCADA network into multiple segments prevents attackers from moving horizontally through the entire system. Organizations can reduce the threat of complete system compromise by keeping network segments which handle critical processes distinct from those used for administration.

Access Control Mechanisms: The least privilege principle in access controls limits user permission to only necessary functions that match their assigned roles. Organizations protect themselves from insider threats through ongoing evaluations and modifications of user access permissions.

Patch Management: Regular software and firmware updates are essential to protect systems from security threats by addressing known vulnerabilities. The establishment of prompt patch management systems for security updates of SCADA elements stands as an essential responsibility for organizations.

Backup and Recovery Plans: Frequent data backups and comprehensive recovery strategies enable organizations to minimize the impact of ransomware attacks and other security breaches. Organizations must evaluate their recovery plans through regular testing to ensure they function properly during emergency events.

Conclusion: To safeguard SCADA systems organizations must possess thorough understanding of current cyber threats.

Analyzing threats to SCADA systems reveals an advanced collection of dangers that change constantly over time. Organizations must gain knowledge about threat characteristics and origins to protect critical infrastructure effectively.

Actual cyber-attack cases examined in this chapter demonstrate why organizations require both proactive and comprehensive cybersecurity strategies. Through integration of risk assessments with employee training and incident response planning together with continuous monitoring organizations can strengthen their cyber defenses.

The following chapters explore protective strategies and frameworks essential for SCADA system security. This section explores how organizations can merge risk management strategies and incident response procedures with emerging technologies to tackle current cybersecurity issues.

A security-focused team-based environment helps organizations defend against current threats while preparing for future risks. Knowing cyber threats to SCADA allows us to unify our protective measures to strengthen critical infrastructure security and safeguard important modern society services.

Appendix: Resources for Further Learning

Readers can obtain extensive information on cybersecurity threats and SCADA system safeguards through these materials.

NIST Cybersecurity Framework: This complete resource helps organizations improve their cybersecurity practices while simultaneously safeguarding essential critical infrastructure systems.

NIST Cybersecurity Framework

Industrial Control Systems Cyber Emergency Response Team (ICS-CERT): The Industrial Control Systems Cyber Emergency Response Team (ICS-CERT) offers support materials to improve security measures for industrial control systems.

ICS-CERT

SANS Institute: The SANS Institute working with ICS-CERT provides educational sessions and materials that cover cybersecurity principles and SCADA security training.

SANS Institute

Cybersecurity and Infrastructure Security Agency (CISA): The Cybersecurity and Infrastructure Security Agency (CISA) delivers complete information that helps secure critical infrastructure against cyber threats.

CISA

Books on SCADA Security: Specialized texts about SCADA security expand your knowledge by covering both security practices and incident response strategies.

Organizations can strengthen their security posture by learning about emerging threats and effective security methods through available resources while they respond to changes.

This section presents risk evaluation frameworks specifically designed for SCADA systems.

Chapter 3: Risk Assessment and Management for SCADA Systems

The previous chapter analyzed various cyber attacks targeted at SCADA systems and explained attacker objectives. Organizations must develop formal risk assessment and management procedures to mitigate risks once they identify potential threats. The chapter analyzes risk assessment principles and practices customized for SCADA systems together with the specific methodologies developed for such environments. In this section we explore how organizations need to establish their security priorities upon identifying potential risks.

Understanding Risk in SCADA Systems

System vulnerabilities create openings which threats can exploit resulting in risk transforming into potential loss or damage. Multiple risks arise from operational disruptions in SCADA systems creating safety concerns as well as financial and reputational harm. The nature of SCADA systems functioning in critical infrastructure necessitates real-time performance which in turn requires extensive risk management approaches.

The Risk Assessment Process

Completing risk assessment requires several essential steps throughout the process.

Asset Identification

Threat Identification

Vulnerability Assessment

Risk Analysis

Risk Evaluation

Risk Treatment

Let's explore each step in detail.

1. Asset Identification

The risk assessment process starts by identifying essential elements within the SCADA system. This includes:

Hardware: Servers, workstations, network devices, RTUs, and PLCs.

Software: SCADA applications, operating systems, and third-party tools.

Data: Operational data, configuration files, and historical records.

People: The SCADA system access list specifies roles which encompass operators as well as IT personnel and vendor representatives.

The foundational basis for all subsequent risk assessment procedures stems from a comprehensive asset inventory.

2. Threat Identification

Organizations must discover possible threats that could exploit existing SCADA system vulnerabilities. Common threat sources include:

External Threats: Cybercriminals, hacktivists, state-sponsored actors, and opportunistic hackers.

Internal Threats: SCADA systems face internal threats when malicious employees and careless staff members or contractors intentionally damage them.

Environmental Threats: Natural disasters, equipment failures, and power outages.

A systematic analysis process is essential for threat documentation to review previous incidents and current developments.

3. Vulnerability Assessment

SCADA systems require vulnerability assessment when potential threats come to light. Vulnerabilities may arise from:

Software Flaws: SCADA system vulnerabilities arise through software bugs and system misconfigurations which exist within system software, firmware, and operating systems.

Weak Access Controls: SCADA systems become highly susceptible to security breaches when they continue to utilize default passwords and lack multi-factor authentication mechanisms.

Insecure Network Configurations: Attackers can move freely across network components in systems that lack adequate network segmentation.

Lack of Employee Training: Insufficient awareness of cybersecurity practices among staff.

Identifying system weaknesses requires effective vulnerability assessments that combine manual testing techniques with automated tools. To protect against security breaches businesses, need to execute regular vulnerability scans and penetration tests.

4. Risk Analysis

Risk analysis examines the probability of identified threats exploiting system faults along with potential damage outcomes. Organizations have the option of applying qualitative methods or quantitative techniques during their risk analysis processes.

Qualitative Risk Analysis: Risk assessment strategies rely upon individual judgments to determine risk levels. Security experts work together with stakeholders to determine risk levels and categorize them as high, medium or low.

Quantitative Risk Analysis: Numerical data measurement serves as the basis for quantitative risk assessment techniques to determine risk levels. Organizations evaluate financial impacts by examining recovery costs together with operational downtime expenses and potential regulatory penalties.

Organizations use risk analysis to create vulnerability prioritization lists by evaluating how operations and safety could potentially be impacted.

5. Risk Evaluation

Following risk analysis organizations evaluate risks by measuring them against pre-established risk appetite and tolerance thresholds. Risk appetite defines the amount of risk that an organization will accept whereas risk tolerance establishes the acceptable variations in risk outcomes.

During this evaluation, organizations may consider:

Regulatory Requirements: Compliance standards that dictate minimum security measures.

Organizational Goals: Business objectives that may influence risk tolerance.

Stakeholder Expectations: Stakeholder expectations become clear through the security practice concerns raised by customers, partners and community members.

Organizations at this level can identify high-priority risks that require immediate attention while simultaneously spotting risks that should be monitored over time.

6. Risk Treatment

Finalizing the risk assessment process requires the development of a risk treatment plan. The risk mitigation plan details multiple strategies to address identified risks by using different approaches.

Risk Avoidance: Business operations producing excessive risk levels must be discontinued or transformed by organizations. Business systems require the removal of outdated software that lacks security patches to maintain system protection.

Risk Reduction: Security measures implementation leads to reduced risk occurrences and lessened potential impacts. The use of intrusion detection systems (IDS) which analyze network traffic enables organizations to reduce their risk exposure by identifying harmful activities.

Risk Transfer: Through the acquisition of insurance policies and management contracts with vendors organizations can transfer risk associated with SCADA system components to third parties.

Risk Acceptance: Organizations sometimes decide to accept specific risks when the potential impact remains minimal, and the mitigation expenses surpass the potential benefits. An organization may opt against deploying comprehensive security protocols to a legacy system which will be retired shortly.

Developing a Risk Treatment Plan

Developing a risk treatment plan requires the identification of actions and the designation of responsible parties. This plan should include:

Specific Actions: Define the security measures to be employed including firewall installation, access control improvements, and regular security training sessions.

Timeline: Set implementation deadlines for the identified actions while considering the urgency of each risk.

Responsible Parties: Designate specific people or groups who will be responsible for completing each task listed in the action plan. This ensures clarity in responsibility and accountability.

Monitoring and Review: Create a timetable to assess how implemented measures perform and to make necessary adjustments to the risk treatment plan. Adapting to changes in the threat landscape requires constant monitoring.

Tools and Frameworks for Risk Assessment

SCADA system risk assessment processes can be enhanced using different tools and frameworks by organizations. Some popular frameworks include:

NIST Special Publication 800-30: The guide outlines a complete risk assessment methodology that includes specific procedures to perform risk evaluations as well as customization techniques for organizational application.

ISO/IEC 27005: This standard outline information security risk management principles while offering guidelines for creating a risk management framework which incorporates risk assessment processes.

CIS Controls: The Center for Internet Security (CIS) offers prioritized cybersecurity best practices which can be applied to both risk assessments and security measures for SCADA systems.

Case Study: Risk Assessment in a SCADA Environment

A water treatment facility's hypothetical case study serves to demonstrate both how risk assessment works and why it is crucial. The water treatment facility uses a SCADA system to handle both monitoring and controlling water quality alongside distribution operations.

Asset Identification

The facility identifies critical assets, including:

Hardware: SCADA servers, RTUs, PLCs, and network switches.

Software: The facility utilizes SCADA applications alongside database management systems and monitoring tools.

Data: Sensor data, operational logs, and configuration files.

People: Operators, IT personnel, and third-party contractors.

Threat Identification

The risk assessment team at the facility identifies potential threats that include:

External Threats: The facility faces threats from cybercriminals who attempt to breach their systems through ransomware attacks or steal sensitive data.

Internal Threats: Employees who have become disgruntled might alter control processes while expropriating confidential information.

Environmental Threats: Physical infrastructure faces possible damage from natural disasters like floods or earthquakes.

Vulnerability Assessment

Through their vulnerability assessment process the team discovers multiple weaknesses.

Outdated Software: Certain SCADA components operate with outdated software that possesses well-documented vulnerabilities.

Weak Access Controls: Default password user accounts exist together with inadequate role-based access control mechanisms.

Lack of Training: The operators lack up-to-date training regarding cybersecurity best practices.

Risk Analysis

The team evaluates how probable it is that identified threats will exploit system weaknesses and what effects those exploits will cause. For instance:

Ransomware Attack: The likelihood rating is high because of emerging patterns in cybercriminal behavior. The possible outcome from a successful attack holds a critical rating because it would interrupt water delivery to thousands.

Insider Threat: The facility's likelihood rating for this threat remains at medium because no past incidents have been recorded. The potential impact reaches a high level because a rogue employee could endanger public safety.

Risk Evaluation

During risk evaluation the team compares potential risks with the facility's risk acceptance levels while considering both regulatory standards and stakeholder expectations. The team decides that immediate measures are necessary to address the ransomware risk while monitoring the insider threat on an ongoing basis.

Risk Treatment Plan

The facility creates its risk treatment strategy which contains the following specific steps:

Immediate Actions: The facility will update outdated software immediately alongside establishing multifactor authentication and launching cybersecurity awareness training for employees.

Long-term Strategies: The organization should create and execute an incident response strategy while establishing continuous vulnerability management practices and performing regular risk evaluation exercises.

Conclusion: The Importance of Ongoing Risk Management

Risk management and assessment require sustained focus with ongoing adjustments to adapt to evolving situations. Organizations need to continuously adjust their risk assessments and security protocols in response to emerging threats and technological progress.

Organizations can protect their SCADA systems against cyber threats and maintain reliable and secure critical infrastructure by adopting a structured risk management approach. The upcoming chapters examine precise methods for incident response and employee training as well as the deployment of cutting-edge security technologies which improve SCADA systems' resilience against an escalating cyber threat landscape.

Moving Forward

The journey through "Beyond the Firewall" requires us to remember that protecting SCADA systems requires everyone to take responsibility. Organizations that create a security-focused work environment with collaborative efforts enable their employees to actively protect essential infrastructure systems. The subsequent chapters are dedicated to examining targeted strategies and best practices for organizations to strengthen their SCADA security frameworks.

Chapter 4: Incident Detection and Response Planning

Incident detection and response planning holds critical importance in SCADA security management. Organizations need to establish rapid and effective procedures to identify and address threats because cyber incidents can have severe consequences. This chapter covers the essential elements of an incident response plan and outlines the specific duties of incident response teams along with the steps organizations need to follow when managing cybersecurity incidents.

The Importance of Incident Detection

Identifying security incidents serves as the primary protective measure against cyber threats. Identifying anomalies or unauthorized activities early in the process aids in minimizing the effects of security breaches. Organizations need to deploy these specific strategies to achieve effective incident detection.

1. Continuous Monitoring

Continuous monitoring requires real-time analysis of network traffic alongside system logs and user activities to detect suspicious behavior. Organizations have access to a suite of tools and technologies which they can deploy to enhance their operations.

Security Information and Event Management (SIEM): SIEM systems collect and examine security data from multiple organizational sources to detect potential security threats. Security teams receive alerts for anomalous access patterns through a SIEM system which may signal a security breach.

Intrusion Detection Systems (IDS): IDS solutions function by observing network traffic to detect known attack patterns and notify administrators about potential security breaches. IDS solutions detect unauthorized access attempts to SCADA systems which allow for prompt responses.

Anomaly Detection Tools: These tools use machine learning and statistical analysis methods to detect behavioral deviations from established norms. An anomaly detection system identifies and flags unusual activities when a user who normally accesses the SCADA system during business hours tries to log in at 2 AM.

2. Log Management

Incident detection depends on maintaining an effective log management system. Organizations need to implement logging procedures that gather and store log data from vital SCADA system components for analysis.

Network Devices: Firewall, router, and switch logs reveal information about network behavior as well as security threats.

SCADA Applications: System behavior anomalies including unauthorized data changes manifest in application logs.

User Activity Logs: User activity monitoring enables organizations to detect suspicious behavior through identification of atypical login attempts and unauthorized access to sensitive data.

The use of a centralized log management system enables better log analysis and boosts the effectiveness of incident detection procedures.

Developing an Incident Response Plan

Organizations need a comprehensive-incident response plan to steer their response procedures during cyber incidents. The response plan must define actionable steps as well as specify roles and communication procedures. The essential elements that make up an incident response plan consist of:

1. Preparation

Successful incident response requires a solid foundation that preparation establishes. This includes:

Incident Response Team (IRT): A crucial phase in preparing for incident response involves forming a team dedicated to managing cybersecurity incidents. The team should include professionals who specialize in IT security, legal matters, communications strategies, and operational functions.

Training and Awareness: The organization needs to conduct uninterrupted training sessions for incident response team members and employees to make sure everyone knows their duties during a cybersecurity incident.

Incident Response Policies and Procedures: Develop written protocols that delineate the strategies for detecting cybersecurity incidents and the subsequent actions needed to address and recover from them. The guidelines should establish clear procedures for escalating incidents based on their severity levels.

2. Identification

Responders must detect potential incidents while evaluating their characteristics and extent during the identification phase. Key activities in this phase include:

Analyzing Alerts: Monitoring tools such as SIEM systems and IDS trigger alerts that initiate the response process. To establish if an alert represents a real incident or a false positive analysts need to examine the context of each alert.

Gathering Evidence: Incident assessment requires analysts to collect both relevant data and system logs to evaluate the extent of the spread. For evidence preservation to enable later analysis teams need to isolate systems that the incident has affected.

3. Containment

Once an incident receives validation the focus shifts to containment processes which aim to prevent further damage. Containment strategies can be categorized into:

Short-Term Containment: Immediate interventions were implemented to lessen the impact of the incident. Organizations need to disconnect their infected systems from the network to prevent malware from spreading further.

Long-Term Containment: While organizations prepare their complete remediation strategy, they should implement temporary fixes and workarounds to keep operations running. Containment procedures may require system updates through patches and access restrictions for compromised components.

4. Eradication

Organizations need to resolve the root cause following the implementation of containment procedures. This may involve:

Removing Malware: Organizations need to employ antivirus and anti-malware solutions to delete all harmful programs present on their systems.

Addressing Vulnerabilities: The organization needs to apply security updates to repair vulnerabilities that caused the incident. To mitigate vulnerabilities organizations can implement security patches or alternatively adjust system configurations and access control settings.

5. Recovery

The recovery phase involves organizations restoring their systems to normal operational status. Key activities include:

System Restoration: System restoration during the recovery phase involves rebuilding systems from clean backups or installing new software copies. System backups must stay clean from corruption and malware during recovery operations to maintain reliable system functionality.

Monitoring for Recurrence: Organizations should closely watch restored systems for indications of recurrent issues. System performance and user activity monitoring is necessary to detect suspicious anomalies which could signal residual threats.

6. Lessons Learned

Incident response completion demands a detailed investigation of the incident together with an assessment of the response measures that were executed. Key activities include:

Post-Incident Review: The incident response team along with relevant stakeholders should convene to analyze the incident details and determine effective actions alongside improvement areas. The review process should focus on analyzing the incident's timeline alongside response effectiveness and evaluating how the organization was affected.

Documentation: Create comprehensive records of incidents which incorporate detailed timelines alongside descriptions of actions executed and results. The documentation created both improves future response strategies and meets regulatory compliance and audit obligations.

Updating Policies and Procedures: Based on their post-incident review outcomes organizations should update their incident response policies and procedures. In response to changes in communication protocols organizations need to upgrade their training materials and enhance their monitoring systems.

Roles and Responsibilities in Incident Response

A response team performs incident response operations effectively when members understand their specific roles and responsibilities. Key roles may include:

Incident Response Manager: The Incident Response Manager handles all aspects of the response operation by leading the team and keeping executive leadership along with stakeholders informed.

Security Analysts: Security analysts monitor systems and analyze alerts while they carry out investigations and assist with incident containment and eradication.

IT Support Staff: IT Support Staff perform technical remediation tasks through system restoration, patch application and security control implementation.

Legal Counsel: Legal Counsel guides organizations through their legal obligations and possible liabilities which emerge from regulatory requirements throughout the incident response process.

Public Relations/Communications Team: The Public Relations/Communications Team manages all communications with both internal parties and the public during the incident to ensure message clarity and factual accuracy while protecting the organization's reputation.

Integrating Incident Response with SCADA Operations

Organizations need to integrate incident response planning with their operational processes because SCADA systems possess distinctive features. This involves:

Collaboration with Operations: Response plans developed with input from operational staff become better aligned with actual operational constraints and conditions. Training exercises need to involve operators to teach them how to execute proper response protocols.

Understanding Operational Priorities: Organizations can effectively prioritize their incident response activities when they understand the essential role SCADA systems play. Response plans need to assess the potential impact of a security breach on both public safety systems and uninterrupted service delivery.

Maintaining Operational Resilience: SCADA operations continue functioning during incidents by implementing resilience strategies that include redundant systems and backup power supplies. Robust system resilience serves as the foundation for maintaining essential services like water supply and power generation.

Conclusion: The Necessity of Preparedness

A fully developed SCADA security framework needs to incorporate incident detection and response planning to adapt to the evolving threat environment. Organizations improve their ability to detect and recover from incidents through proactive incident response frameworks.

The upcoming segment of "Beyond the Firewall" will explore further SCADA security enhancements through advanced technology deployment and employee training while developing a robust cybersecurity culture. A comprehensive strategy will emerge from the collaboration of these components to safeguard essential systems against future cyber threats.

Chapter 5: Employee Training and Awareness Programs

Despite the necessity of strong technological security measures for SCADA system protection, the human element plays a key role in maintaining cybersecurity. Both employees and contractors as well as third-party vendors may introduce system vulnerabilities that affect critical infrastructure through unintentional errors or intentional actions. A complete employee training and awareness program stands as an essential requirement to improve SCADA security rather than being just a recommended best practice. This chapter examines how employee training plays a vital role in SCADA security and details the necessary elements of successful training programs while suggesting methods to establish a strong security-focused culture in organizations operating SCADA systems.

Human factors play an essential role in maintaining SCADA security.

Modern SCADA systems' interconnected framework combined with rising remote access and cloud technology use broadens the possible attack surface. The larger attack surface now present raises the chances that human mistakes will turn into important security weaknesses. Employees can unknowingly become targets of phishing attacks when they click harmful links or download infected files. Weak password enforcement can leave accounts open to brute-force attacks because employees fail to follow strong password practices. When employees ignore suspicious activities, they delay the security team's ability to detect and respond to potential breaches.

To grasp SCADA security from a human perspective requires awareness of multiple factors.

Social Engineering: Social engineering tactics enable attackers to manipulate employees into disclosing sensitive information or taking actions that undermine security by exploiting human psychology through methods like phishing emails and pretexting calls.

Negligence and Lack of Awareness: Good employees can cause security risks through unintentional carelessness when they fail to follow cybersecurity best practices. Insignificant mistakes such as selecting weak passwords or neglecting software updates can lead to serious security issues.

Insider Threats: Although rare, employees or contractors who misuse their authorized access represent a major security risk. Employees authorized to access systems have deep system insights which allow them to inflict substantial damage or extract confidential information.

To protect against cybersecurity risks organizations, need training programs that prepare employees to understand vulnerabilities and develop skills necessary for operating securely in cyber environments.

Designing Effective Training Programs: A Multi-Layered Approach

SCADA security training programs require customization rather than using a generic approach. The training program requires customization to address the distinct roles and responsibilities each employee holds in the organization. The training program requires multiple layers through different methods to improve knowledge retention and increase participant engagement.

1. Baseline Cybersecurity Awareness Training

Foundational training must be required for every employee across all levels of technical knowledge. It should cover fundamental cybersecurity concepts, including:

Understanding Cyber Threats: The training familiarizes employees with different cyber threats including malware attacks as well as phishing schemes and ransomware along with denial-of-service attacks. Case studies and practical examples help make training more engaging while demonstrating its real-world applicability.

Password Security Best Practices: Organizations must provide training to employees about generating strong passwords for each account and teach them how password managers can be used effectively. Organizations need to educate their staff about the risks of password reuse together with the necessity to maintain proper password hygiene.

Phishing and Social Engineering Awareness: The implementation of this security measure plays a vital role in protecting organizations from social engineering threats. Training programs must demonstrate practical examples of phishing emails and smishing (SMS phishing) techniques along with vishing (voice phishing) attacks. Organizations must educate their employees about recognizing suspicious emails and messages and making proper reports when they encounter suspicious phone calls.

Safe Browsing Habits: Training should teach employees safe browsing habits that involve steering clear of suspicious websites while utilizing HTTPS connections and maintaining caution when downloading files from untrusted sources.

Data Security and Confidentiality: The module must emphasize data protection and compliance with organizational data handling and storage policies. Staff members must be aware of their data confidentiality duties and understand what happens when data breaches occur.

Reporting Procedures: Organizations need well-defined procedures which employees can use to report suspicious activities and security incidents. The company must create an environment that enables employees to report concerns freely without any concern about facing retaliation. The reporting process needs to function without complexity and remain available to all users.

2. Role-Based Training

Organizations need to develop role-specific training programs that address the unique job functions of their employees beyond basic training requirements. For instance:

SCADA Operators: Operators must learn about cybersecurity threats that affect SCADA system operations. The training should address system monitoring processes alongside methods for detecting anomalies and incident response procedures and emphasize maintaining system integrity. Practical simulations and hands-on training exercises provide significant benefits within this instructional framework.

IT Personnel: IT professionals need additional advanced training concerning security technologies and practices used with SCADA systems. This training will encompass network security practices along with vulnerability management techniques and methods for intrusion detection and incident response procedures. Relevant certifications like CompTIA Security+, CISSP or GICSP work to boost professional expertise.

Management and Leadership: Training programs for management and leadership personnel must emphasize their roles in creating a culture attentive to security and managing resources dedicated to cybersecurity projects. This training program includes risk management strategies, incident response planning techniques, compliance regulations and the importance of building a workplace security awareness culture.

3. Regular Refresher Training and Updates

Cybersecurity threats are constantly evolving. Employees must receive periodic refresher training to stay informed about evolving threats and best practices. Refresher training sessions need to strengthen fundamental concepts learned previously while presenting employees with the latest information about new cybersecurity threats and technological developments. The training sessions should provide employees with chances to ask questions and examine practical situations.

4. Utilizing Diverse Training Methods

Organizations can boost employee retention of information and participation by implementing multiple training approaches that include:

Interactive Workshops: Employees have the chance to participate actively in these workshops while they can ask questions and join discussions. Interactive workshops help employees learn about phishing protection, social engineering defenses and secure web browsing practices.

Online Modules: Online training modules provide employees with flexible access to training materials which they can review according to their own schedule. These learning modules serve to strengthen fundamental understanding while offering additional insights about subjects.

Simulated Phishing Attacks: Simulated phishing attacks train employees to recognize and report suspicious emails. These exercises simulate real-world situations that emphasize the significance of maintaining vigilance and practicing email security measures.

Gamification: The use of game-like elements in training programs boosts both participant engagement and their ability to retain information. Learning through gamified training modules becomes both more fun and effective for users.

Case Studies and Real-World Examples: Training becomes more effective and relevant when real-world cyber incidents are used as examples. Through case studies organizations can see the negative results of weak security procedures and realize why staying alert is crucial.

Fostering a Culture of Security Awareness

A comprehensive security program includes effective training together with multiple other components. Organizations can achieve true SCADA security enhancement only when they establish a culture that recognizes security as a joint responsibility for all members. Leadership must take active measures while engaging employees at every level throughout their work routine.

Leadership Commitment: Setting the Tone

Leadership establishes essential cybersecurity guidelines that shape organizational policies. The leadership must demonstrate their support for security measures by sponsoring essential training and awareness programs through proper resource allocation. Organizational leaders must take part in security operations and inform staff about security importance while enforcing security policy compliance.

Communication and Engagement: Keeping Security Top of Mind

Consistent communication plays a critical role in ensuring staff awareness and strengthening security best practices. Security updates, tips, and reminders must be distributed through multiple communication channels including newsletters, email announcements, and internal messaging platforms by organizations. Interactive quizzes together with short videos and infographics enhance the accessibility and engagement of security information.

Incentives and Recognition: Promoting Proactive Behavior

Organizations that identify and reward workers for their proactive security actions will strengthen their security culture. Organizations can promote proactive security behavior through incentives for suspicious activity reporting, participation in training programs and suggestions for security enhancements. Recognizing employees who enhance organizational security publicly helps build a positive and supportive workplace environment.

Continuous Improvement: Adapting to Evolving Threats

The cybersecurity landscape is constantly changing. Organizations need to persistently evaluate and enhance their training programs to stay aligned with emerging threats and industry best practices. Organizations can maintain relevant and effective training programs by conducting regular assessments of training effectiveness and collecting employee feedback for necessary improvements.

Conclusion: A Human-Centric Approach to SCADA Security

Although technological safeguards are vital for SCADA security protection technology alone is not enough because human factors play an essential role. Organizations should view employee training programs as essential investments to improve their security posture rather than just meeting compliance standards. Organizations can prepare their employees to defend SCADA systems against constantly changing cyber threats by implementing a security-focused culture alongside regular training and diverse educational techniques. The integration of a human-centered security strategy with strong technological defenses establishes a reliable foundation for SCADA system protection. The subsequent chapter examines essential network security practices to safeguard communication channels in SCADA systems.

Chapter 6: Network security methods for SCADA systems through network segmentation and access control

Earlier sections highlighted how SCADA security requires multiple layers including human factors, incident response planning, and thorough employee training. This chapter examines the protection of network infrastructure which functions as essential connections between different SCADA system components. Maintaining strong network security is essential because of the sensitive nature of transmitted data and the severe impact that data breaches can have. This chapter analyzes essential methods for protecting SCADA networks which involve implementing network segmentation alongside access control mechanisms and the secure deployment of different network protocols.

The Unique Challenges of SCADA Network Security

Security experts face distinct challenges when protecting SCADA networks. SCADA systems differ from traditional IT networks because they:

Legacy Systems: SCADA systems frequently use legacy equipment and software which lack essential security features or are inherently difficult to update. Attackers can leverage significant vulnerabilities within SCADA systems because they use legacy systems.

Proprietary Protocols: SCADA systems use proprietary communication protocols which frequently lack the extensive vetting or documentation found in standard protocols. The absence of standardization complicates the detection and resolution of security weaknesses.

Real-Time Requirements: The nature of SCADA systems requires immediate response times which necessitate extremely low communication delays. Real-time performance requirements limit security measure implementation options because such measures can increase communication latency.

Physical Proximity: SCADA components frequently operate in exposed physical locations including substations and industrial facilities. Because SCADA components are often located in physically exposed locations there exists an increased risk of unauthorized physical access which attackers can exploit to compromise the system.

Interconnectivity: The increased integration of modern SCADA systems with IT networks creates broader opportunities for potential attacks. The interconnected nature of modern systems allows attackers to move across IT networks and access SCADA systems.

Network Segmentation: Isolate and Protect

Implementing network segmentation provides essential protection for SCADA systems. The practice of network segmentation divides networks into smaller segments which remain isolated from each other to reduce the effect of any security breach. Once an attacker breaches one network segment, they face significant barriers to reaching other essential system parts. Successful SCADA network segmentation depends on meticulous planning and assessment of its system components.

Defining Zones and Levels

The Purdue Model provides a typical method for network segmentation by establishing five distinct levels for industrial automation systems. Every level corresponds to distinct zones that have unique security requirements.

Level 0: Level 0 represents the process level that includes sensors along with actuators and various field devices. The security requirements for this level are the strictest and we must limit network connectivity to the bare minimum.

Level 1: Basic control level, encompassing PLCs and RTUs. The basic control level must implement strong security measures to deter unauthorized access.

Level 2: The supervisory control level functions as the monitoring and control center for industrial processes. The Supervisory Control Level demands strong security protocols to safeguard control systems from unauthorized access and manipulation.

Level 3: The data acquisition level serves to aggregate data from multiple levels for analysis purposes. Security protocols must prioritize the protection of data integrity and confidentiality.

Level 4: Enterprise level systems integrate SCADA networks with company business systems and corporate networks. Strong security controls must be implemented at this stage to block attacker movements from business networks into SCADA networks.

The separation between each network level must be achieved through the implementation of firewalls and intrusion detection systems alongside various security mechanisms.

Implementing Segmentation

Implementing network segmentation involves:

Firewalls: Place firewalls between network layers to limit traffic movement.

VLANs (Virtual LANs): Network segments can be logically divided using VLANs even when they exist on a single physical infrastructure.

Network Access Control (NAC): Using NAC solutions enables network access management by verifying device identity and security posture. Connection to the SCADA network should be restricted to devices that have proper authorization and meet security standards.

DMZs (Demilitarized Zones): The establishment of DMZs helps to separate non-critical components from the main SCADA network infrastructure.

Access Control Mechanisms: Limiting Access to Authorized Users

Access control represents a fundamental element of SCADA network security. Network access control restricts access to resources by enforcing the least privilege principle (PoLP). Users should receive access limited to what they need to fulfill their job responsibilities according to this principle. Organizations reduce the damage from compromised accounts by restricting access permissions.

Implementing Access Control

Effective access control involves:

Strong Authentication: Organizations should adopt robust authentication processes including multi-factor authentication (MFA) to verify user identities. MFA protects user accounts by making users provide several authentication methods including both a password and a one-time code.

Role-Based Access Control (RBAC): Users receive predefined permissions when assigned to established roles. Access limitations guarantee that sensitive data and functions remain available only to authorized users.

Regular Access Reviews: Regular evaluations and adjustments of user access permissions maintain their relevance and appropriateness. The system protects against unauthorized access while making sure users can only reach necessary resources.

Account Management: Robust account management procedures must include regular password changes along with account lockouts following multiple failed logins attempts and immediate account deactivation when employees depart the organization.

Network Intrusion Detection and Prevention Systems (NIDPS): Implement NIDPS solutions to track network traffic patterns that identify malicious activity and block unauthorized access attempts. These systems have the capability to identify threats and block them before they reach essential SCADA components.

Secure Implementation of Network Protocols

SCADA systems depend on multiple communication protocols to facilitate data transfer between system components. Network integrity depends on the secure implementation of these communication protocols. Organizations need to add extra security measures because many protocols lack built-in security features.

Common SCADA Protocols and Security Considerations:

Modbus: Modbus is a prevalent industrial automation protocol which does not include security features within its structure. Organizations need to add security measures including encryption and access control to safeguard Modbus communications. Unless necessary and appropriately secured

Modbus TCP/IP should be substituted with more secure communication protocols.

DNP3 (Distributed Network Protocol 3): DNP3 provides superior security features compared to Modbus because it includes authentication and encryption capabilities. Effective security requires correct configuration and implementation practices. Outdated versions of DNP3 should be avoided.

OPC UA (OLE for Process Control Unified Architecture): OPC UA represents a modern security-focused protocol created for industrial automation applications. The protocol includes inherent security functions that provide authentication and encryption capabilities together with digital signatures. The OPC UA protocol provides better security than legacy protocols like Modbus.

PROFINET: The industrial Ethernet protocol PROFINET finds widespread application in automation systems. PROFINET includes strong security mechanisms such as authentication and encryption alongside access control which positions it as an ideal option for protecting SCADA networks.

Ethernet/IP: The industrial Ethernet protocol Ethernet/IP includes security features that match those found in PROFINET. When implementing Ethernet/IP it is necessary to establish appropriate security measures.

Securing these protocols often involves:

Encryption: Protect data confidentiality and integrity through encrypted communication methods. The system maintains data protection against unauthorized access even when network security breaks down.

Authentication: Implementing authentication mechanisms enables verification of identities for devices that communicate with each other. Unauthorized devices cannot access the SCADA network because of this security measure.

Authorization: Establishing access control lists (ACLs) to limit device actions ensure security by defining what operations devices can execute. Access control lists restrict device actions to those which have received proper authorization.

Wireless Communication Security

SCADA systems now frequently employ wireless communication because it provides deployment flexibility alongside ease of operation. The nature of wireless networks makes them vulnerable to security risks because signals can be broadcast and intercepted by unauthorized parties. Securing wireless communication requires:

Strong Encryption: Protect wireless data by deploying strong encryption methods such as WPA2 or WPA3.

Access Control: Deploy access control systems that restrict wireless network entry. Security measures include MAC address filtering and strong password configuration.

Regular Security Audits: Perform regular security audits on the wireless network to spot and resolve potential vulnerabilities.

Physical Security: Putting physical protections in place that prevent unauthorized individuals from reaching wireless access points.

Network Monitoring and Threat Detection

The SCADA network requires constant surveillance to enable quick detection and response to security incidents. This involves:

Network Monitoring Tools: Network monitoring tools enable organizations to track network traffic while identifying anomalies and detecting potential intrusions. These tools deliver real-time network activity insights so organizations can respond to security threats quickly.

Intrusion Detection Systems (IDS): Organizations implement IDS solutions to track network traffic patterns and inform system administrators about potential intrusion attempts.

Security Information and Event Management (SIEM): Security Information and Event Management systems gather and analyze data from multiple sources to deliver a full overview of SCADA network security.

Regular Security Audits: Organizations need to perform routine security audits on their SCADA networks to detect and resolve vulnerabilities. The audits need to cover technical aspects as well as procedural evaluations.

Conclusion: A Holistic Approach to SCADA Network Security

To secure SCADA networks effectively organizations must adopt a comprehensive strategy that includes network segmentation along with strong access controls, secure protocol deployment and persistent monitoring. Organizations need to assess their unique requirements and put proper security practices in place that align with their risk profile. Organizations that develop a comprehensive network security strategy can effectively minimize cyber incident risks and safeguard their critical infrastructure systems. The subsequent chapters explore detailed security technologies alongside strategies that will strengthen SCADA systems security.

Chapter 7: Securing Remote Access to SCADA Systems

SCADA systems now depend more on remote access which creates potential benefits and substantial security risks. Remote access allows for effective supervision and upkeep of scattered assets which leads to better operational efficiency and minimized system outages. SCADA systems face increased vulnerability to cyber-attacks because connectivity broadens their attack surface. The chapter examines remote access security risks while outlining best practices for remote connection security and evaluating technologies and strategies for risk reduction.

The Security Implications of Remote Access

The ability to access SCADA systems from remote locations introduces multiple security weaknesses.

Expanded Attack Surface: SCADA network penetration becomes easier because remote access introduces multiple new entry points for attackers. Exploiting any vulnerability in remote access infrastructure enables attackers to access the entire system without authorization.

Increased Vulnerability to Phishing and Social Engineering: The use of email and other communication platforms for connection initiation through remote access heightens the potential for both phishing and social engineering attacks. Through deception attackers can manipulate users to expose their login information or install harmful software that provides them with entry to the SCADA network.

Difficulty in Monitoring and Controlling Access: Remote access management presents complexity because organizations struggle to track authorized users and their permitted activities.

Insufficient visibility leads to higher chances of unauthorized access and malicious activities remaining unnoticed.

Vulnerabilities in Remote Access Technologies: Remote access technologies including VPNs and remote desktop protocols contain vulnerabilities which attackers can exploit. Attackers can utilize improperly configured remote access technologies as entry points when these systems lack proper maintenance.

Data Exposure: Sensitive operational data could be accessed unlawfully due to remote access. Attackers can intercept and exploit unprotected data during transmission.

Best Practices for Securing Remote Access

Protecting remote SCADA system access demands multiple layers of security technologies and practices.

1. Virtual Private Networks (VPNs): Establishing Secure Connections

VPNs establish secure encrypted pathways between remote users and the SCADA network to safeguard data being sent during remote connections. The following points should guide your choice of VPN solution:

Strong Encryption: Utilize strong encryption algorithms like AES-256 within your VPN to maintain data confidentiality.

Authentication Mechanisms: Create strong authentication systems like multi-factor authentication (MFA) to validate user identities securely. MFA protects user accounts by adding multiple authentication steps through which users must provide different verification methods including passwords and one-time code.

Access Control: Deploy access control lists (ACLs) to limit resource access within the SCADA network to designated users.

Access to network resources must be limited to what users need to perform their respective job functions.

Regular Updates: It's crucial to update VPN software and firmware regularly to fix any known security flaws.

Centralized Management: Implement a centralized VPN management solution for easier administration and monitoring.

2. Multi-Factor Authentication (MFA): Enhancing Security

Multi-Factor Authentication (MFA) provides additional security protection above traditional password-only authentication systems. The system demands that users complete multiple authentication steps to confirm their identity thereby creating substantial hurdles for attackers trying to gain unauthorized access. Different MFA methods include:

One-Time Passwords (OTPs): Generated by authentication apps or hardware tokens.

Biometrics: Biometric systems authenticate users by analyzing physical characteristics like fingerprints or facial features.

Hardware Security Keys: Utilizing physical security keys which create unique codes for each login session.

3. Jump Servers: Secure Access to Internal Networks

Jump servers function as access points to internal networks while providing entry to SCADA systems. They enhance security by:

Reducing Direct Exposure: Users reduce exposure risks because they connect to a jump server before accessing critical SCADA components directly.

Centralized Access Control: The access management process becomes simpler because access to the jump server can be strictly regulated.

Auditing and Monitoring: The jump server provides a straightforward solution for monitoring and auditing system activity.

4. Remote Desktop Protocols (RDP): Secure Configuration

Windows-based systems generally use RDP for remote access. To secure RDP connections:

Strong Passwords: Enforce strong password policies for RDP accounts.

Network Level Authentication (NLA): Activate NLA to secure communication between the client machine and the server.

Restrict Access: Authorized users and specific IP addresses should be granted exclusive access to RDP.

Regular Updates: Keep the RDP server software up to date.

5. Secure Shell (SSH): A Secure Alternative for Linux/Unix Systems

The SSH protocol offers secure access to systems running Linux and Unix. It offers robust encryption and authentication capabilities which makes SSH a more secure choice than RDP for these systems. To enhance SSH security:

Strong Authentication: Combine strong authentication methods with password-based authentication by adding public key authentication.

Key Management: Adopt strong key management procedures to ensure private key protection.

Restrict Access: Restrict SSH entry points to specific authorized users and designated IP addresses.

Regular Updates: Keep the SSH server software up to date.

6. Regular security audits and penetration tests help reveal vulnerabilities in remote access systems.

The remote access infrastructure requires regular security audits and penetration testing to identify vulnerabilities. These assessments should cover:

VPN Configuration: The VPN configuration must be examined to ensure it meets established security standards.

Access Control Lists: The access control lists must be properly set to ensure only authorized users and resources can access them.

Firewall Rules: Firewall rules require proper configuration to block unauthorized access attempts.

Vulnerability Scanning: Security teams employ vulnerability scanners to detect known security weaknesses in remote access systems.

Penetration Testing: Attack simulations mimic real-world threats to uncover potential security weaknesses and evaluate security control performance.

7. Employee Training and Awareness: The Human Element

To reduce remote access risks companies must prioritize employee training and awareness programs. Employees should be trained on:

Secure Remote Access Practices: Employees must learn how to implement strong passwords while using multi-factor authentication along with secure VPN connections.

Phishing and Social Engineering Awareness: Organizations need to educate employees about how to detect and prevent phishing and social engineering attacks.

Reporting Procedures: Create unambiguous protocols for employees to report suspicious activities and security incidents.

8. Network Segmentation: Isolating Remote Access Networks

The practice of segmenting networks serves to contain damage from successful cyber-attacks. Organizations can protect their critical systems from easy attacks by keeping the remote access network separate from the core SCADA network. Network segmentation can be implemented using firewalls and VLANs alongside other segmentation methods.

9. Data Loss Prevention (DLP): Protecting Sensitive Data

Through network monitoring and control measures, DLP solutions block unauthorized data exfiltration of sensitive information. The system watches both network traffic and data storage to detect and stop unauthorized data exfiltration efforts. It becomes particularly crucial to secure SCADA systems because they generally store vital operational information.

10. Monitoring and Logging: Maintaining Visibility

Security incidents require both comprehensive monitoring and logging to ensure effective detection and response. Organizations need to track VPN connections alongside user activity and system logs to detect suspicious behavior. The collected information provides essential insights for examining security incidents and enhancing organizational security measures.

Technologies for Secure Remote Access

Multiple technologies exist to improve remote access protection for SCADA systems.

Next-Generation Firewalls (NGFWs): Next-Generation Firewalls deliver enhanced security for remote access connections through features including intrusion prevention systems, application control measures and malware detection tools.

Intrusion Detection/Prevention Systems (IDS/IPS): IDS/IPS systems scan network traffic to detect malicious activity and respond by either blocking threats or generating alerts thereby improving remote access network protection.

Secure Access Service Edge (SASE): Network security features including secure web gateways, VPNs, and cloud access security brokers (CASBs) combine within a cloud-based service through SASE. The process of managing remote access security becomes more straightforward.

Zero Trust Network Access (ZTNA): ZTNA solutions enable secure access to applications and resources by validating user identity and context irrespective of physical location. Reducing potential vulnerabilities while strengthening security measures takes place through access verification at every connection stage.

Conclusion: A Proactive Approach to Remote Access Security

Protection of remote access to SCADA systems demands active measures and multiple security layers. Organizations that apply strong security protocols including VPNs, MFA, jump servers and regular audits can reduce remote access risks while maintaining enhanced efficiency and accessibility benefits. The human element continues to be essential and comprehensive employee training stands out as vital for avoiding remote access incidents. Protecting SCADA systems from evolving threats requires a holistic security strategy that merges technological safeguards with a strong security culture. The upcoming section investigates how to protect SCADA systems from advanced persistent threats (APTs).

Chapter 8: Advanced Persistent Threats (APTs) and SCADA Security

This section has examined multiple SCADA security elements by examining prevalent threats and outlining best practices with technological solutions. The threat landscape includes more than just attacks that are easy to detect. Advanced Persistent Threats (APTs) stand as an especially dangerous and complex type of cyberattack which creates significant obstacles for SCADA security. This chapter examines APT characteristics and targeting strategies while detailing defensive actions organizations need to take against these enduring targeted cyber threats.

Understanding Advanced Persistent Threats (APTs)

APTs are defined by their ability to remain undetected while maintaining long-term operations that target specific objectives. APTs represent carefully orchestrated attacks that target specific objectives, executed by state-sponsored units or organized crime groups along with expert independent actors who operate beyond the scope of spontaneous, short-term attack strategies. Key characteristics of APTs include:

Stealth and Evasion: Using custom-developed malware and zero-day vulnerability exploitation APTs utilize advanced methods to avoid detection. They aim to stay hidden over long durations because this enables them to collect information and organize their attacks strategically.

Persistence: APT perpetrators develop their tools to keep control of target systems for several years. Organizations maintain covert backdoors that enable them to access systems repeatedly without triggering alerts.

Targeted Attacks: APT attacks prioritize specific organizations and individuals who possess valuable data or control critical infrastructure. Through detailed analysis of their targets the attackers discover security weaknesses to develop customized methods for penetration.

Data Exfiltration: The main purpose of several Advanced Persistent Threats (APTs) is to carry out data exfiltration which means stealing sensitive information from targeted systems without authorization. The stolen data enables attackers to conduct industrial espionage operations while supporting political sabotage activities and achieving financial benefits.

Sophisticated Techniques: Advanced Persistent Threats (APTs) deploy multiple complex methods such as spear-phishing attacks along with watering hole tactics and using malware implants to exploit software weaknesses. Multiple sophisticated techniques merge to form a complex attack chain which resist detection and disruption.

APT Targeting Strategies in SCADA Environments

APT groups target SCADA systems because they manage essential industrial processes and infrastructure operations. Attackers choose SCADA systems as their target for several different purposes.

Industrial Espionage: SCADA systems become targets for competitors or foreign governments because they aim to steal intellectual property along with trade secrets and operational data. Stolen information provides attackers with a substantial competitive edge and detailed understanding of an organization's capabilities.

Sabotage and Disruption: Critical infrastructure can face disruption from state-sponsored actors or terrorist groups targeting SCADA systems which leads to economic damage and social disruption. The severity of attacks on SCADA systems varies from minor disruptions to complete system failures based on the objectives of the attackers.

Cyber Warfare: State-sponsored entities utilize advanced persistent threats to launch cyber-attacks against enemy nations' critical infrastructure with the goal of earning strategic benefits or causing economic damage. Such attacks demonstrate high levels of sophistication which makes them challenging to identify.

Defending Against APTs in SCADA Environments

Organizations must implement an active multi-layered defense strategy that extends past standard security protocols to protect against APTs. Key strategies include:

1. Threat Intelligence: Staying Ahead of the Curve

Organizations must stay current on new threats to mount effective defenses against APTs. Organizations must integrate threat intelligence feeds from government entities, cybersecurity companies, and industry information-sharing organizations. Organizations can use this intelligence to discover potential threats and weaknesses and take proactive steps to establish defensive countermeasures.

2. Limiting lateral movement requires network segmentation alongside strict access controls.

The effectiveness of network segmentation and robust access control measures is crucial to restrict the damage caused by an APT breach. Organizations can protect their SCADA network from lateral attacks by separating critical components into distinct sections. Organizations must implement robust authentication techniques including multi-factor authentication to protect their systems. The principle of least privilege (PoLP) restricts user access to essential privileges necessary for job performance which helps to reduce the risks that arise from account breaches.

3. Intrusion Detection and Prevention Systems (IDS/IPS) function as an Early Warning System to detect and prevent threats.

IDS/IPS solutions are essential tools for detecting and preventing attacks from advanced persistent threats. These systems analyze network traffic to detect malicious activities by identifying suspicious patterns that suggest an APT campaign. Organizations can improve their threat detection and response capabilities through the integration of IDS/IPS technology with SIEM systems and other security tools. Next-generation firewalls (NGFWs) frequently embed sophisticated IDS/IPS functions.

4. Security Information and Event Management (SIEM) systems function as centralized platforms for security monitoring.

SIEM systems function as a central platform that gathers security data from multiple sources and performs analysis and management of this information. Aggregated data allows organizations to obtain complete visibility into their security posture while also identifying suspicious activities. SIEM systems analyze data from multiple sources to discover sophisticated attack patterns that signal APT campaigns. Successful deployment of SIEM systems depends on precise configuration settings, development of correlation rules, and the presence of experienced analysts who can make sense of the massive data volumes produced.

5. Vulnerability Management: Patching and Remediation

Frequent software vulnerability patching and remediation efforts are essential to stop APT attacks. Attackers frequently use known software vulnerabilities to penetrate systems and establish initial access. Organizations must establish a strong vulnerability management program that includes frequent vulnerability scans and patch management along with prompt remediation actions against detected weaknesses. A structured method for vulnerability detection and prioritization followed by appropriate resolution measures needs to consider SCADA systems' operational limitations that function in real time.

6. Endpoint Detection and Response (EDR): Host-Based Security

EDR solutions offer sophisticated detection and response features for threats at the endpoint level. These solutions offer monitoring of system activity to detect malicious behavior which enables organizations to respond to threats that have bypassed network defenses. EDR solutions enable organizations to detect and stop malware while preventing data from leaving the network and capturing forensic data needed for incident response.

7. Threat Hunting: Proactive Threat Detection

Threat hunting requires security professionals to actively search for signs of harmful activity in the network instead of just responding to security alerts. The proactive detection approach proves highly effective against APTs since these threats typically seek to remain hidden. A range of tools and techniques enables threat hunters to detect suspicious activity through network traffic analysis along with log analysis and malware analysis. Professionals must possess advanced skills and specific knowledge to comprehend attacker tactics, techniques, and procedures (TTPs).

8. Security Awareness Training: Human Element Remains Critical

The human element stands as a significant vulnerability despite having strong technological security measures in place. Human error can lead to security breaches when employees unintentionally create vulnerabilities or become targets of social engineering scams. Employees need comprehensive security awareness training to learn about APT risks and the proper way to identify and report unusual activities. The training program needs to teach employees about phishing methods, social engineering strategies and safe internet navigation. Conducting simulated phishing exercises and regular refresher training sessions strengthens these security concepts.

9. Data Loss Prevention (DLP): Preventing Data Exfiltration

Advanced Persistent Threats frequently attempt to extract confidential information from their target systems. DLP solutions protect against unauthorized data transfers by observing both network traffic and data storage areas. DLP solutions detect unauthorized data transfer attempts outside the organization's network and block them to safeguard vital information from unauthorized access. The system needs precise configuration which balances security requirements with operational demands while preventing false alarms that might interfere with legitimate business processes.

10. Continuous improvement requires regular security audits and penetration testing to identify vulnerabilities and assess security control effectiveness.

The essential practice of conducting regular security audits along with penetration testing enables organizations to find vulnerabilities while evaluating their security measures. The assessments need to encompass every segment of the SCADA system from network infrastructure through applications to endpoints. Penetration tests mimic actual attack scenarios to discover system vulnerabilities while testing how well the organization identifies and responds to security threats. The security posture of the SCADA system should benefit from continuous improvements based on assessment results.

Case Study: This case study explores a simulated APT attack against a water treatment facility.

A state-sponsored APT group targets a water treatment facility. The attackers initiate their assault by sending a spear-phishing email to an employee which masquerades as correspondence from a trusted vendor. Opening the email's malicious attachment installs a sophisticated malware implant onto the system.

The malware provides attackers with continuous entry capabilities into the facility's SCADA network. The attackers avoid detection for several months during which they thoroughly map the network and steal sensitive operational data. Using gathered data, attackers design a sophisticated attack that manipulates SCADA system controls to make undetectable water treatment adjustments. The changes caused by the attack do not produce immediate disasters but result in a slow deterioration of water quality that could eventually create health risks for the local population.

The hypothetical scenario demonstrates how APTs operate stealthily and emphasizes the necessity of implementing proactive security measures. The fact that attackers can avoid detection over long periods shows why organizations need threat intelligence along with continuous monitoring and strong security controls.

Conclusion: Proactive and Multi-Layered Defense

SCADA security must contend with the considerable difficulty posed by Advanced Persistent Threats. The stealthy nature of APTs coupled with their long-term persistence and sophisticated attack methods demands organizations to adopt a proactive defense strategy that includes multiple layers of protection. Organizations can protect themselves from highly targeted attacks through robust security measures combined with threat intelligence and a security-conscious organizational culture. The constant development of APT techniques demands an ongoing cycle of security improvement through routine assessments and strategic updates to manage new threats. The upcoming chapter examines how regulatory compliance and industry standards play an essential role in improving SCADA security.

Chapter 9: Compliance, Regulations, and Standards in SCADA Security

Earlier chapters examined different technologies and processes involved in SCADA system protection. Effective SCADA security strategies require both a thorough understanding and strict adherence to applicable compliance regulations and industry standards. This chapter analyzes regulatory compliance significance and investigates the main regulations and standards that affect SCADA security while presenting strategies to achieve and sustain compliance.

Regulatory compliance serves as a fundamental element for establishing effective SCADA security measures.

A strong SCADA security posture requires regulatory compliance which goes beyond penalty avoidance. Mandated compliance requirements lead organizations to install essential security controls which create a safer operational environment. Adhering to compliance standards provides multiple advantages which surpass just avoiding legal fines and consequences.

Enhanced Security Posture: The requirements of compliance regulations include specific security measures such as access control systems, vulnerability management programs and incident response strategies. Compliance with these mandates enhances the defense capabilities of SCADA networks.

Increased Stakeholder Confidence: Building a compliance-oriented approach helps establish stakeholder trust with customers, investors, and regulatory bodies. The strengthened confidence in business relations leads to stronger partnerships between organizations.

Improved Operational Resilience: Organizations must put in place resilience-enhancing measures like redundancy and backup systems to achieve compliance. Enhanced resilience allows organizations to reduce disruption effects while maintaining operational continuity.

Reduced Risk of Data Breaches: Data protection and privacy are common subjects of compliance regulations. Organizations that follow these regulations decrease their vulnerability to data breaches along with the financial and reputational harm that follows.

Proactive Risk Management: Compliance requires organizations to take a proactive risk management approach which involves identifying potential security threats before assessing their severity and implementing mitigation strategies. By taking proactive steps organizations can strengthen their security posture and minimize potential security incidents.

Key Regulations and Standards Impacting SCADA Security

SCADA security regulations and standards differ based on the industry sector, geographical location, and importance of the infrastructure. Some key examples include:

1. The North American Electric Reliability Corporation (NERC) Critical Infrastructure Protection (CIP) Standards represent mandatory reliability requirements for the North American bulk electric system.

NERC CIP standards represent mandatory reliability requirements that all bulk electric systems across North America must follow. The standards require organizations to implement specific security controls to protect the electric power grid from cybersecurity risks.

Access Control: Critical assets must only be accessible to users with the minimum necessary privileges as mandated by the principle of least privilege.

Vulnerability Management: SCADA systems require routine vulnerability detection followed by appropriate corrective action.

Incident Response Planning: Organizations must develop and test plans which will respond to cybersecurity incidents as part of their incident response strategy.

Security Awareness Training: Providing cybersecurity awareness training to employees.

Physical Security: Critical infrastructure protection requires the implementation of physical security measures.

Organizations that do not adhere to NERC CIP standards risk facing heavy fines and penalties.

2. International Organization for Standardization (ISO) 27001:

ISO 27001 stands as a global benchmark standard for information security management systems (ISMS). The standard outlines methods for developing and sustaining an ISMS through continuous improvement and maintenance while covering all areas of information security.

Risk Assessment and Management: Perform regular risk assessments to identify security risks and manage them effectively.

Access Control: Establish strong access control practices to protect sensitive information.

Data Security: Measures to protect data confidentiality along with integrity and availability need to be implemented.

Incident Management: Establishing processes for handling security incidents effectively.

Organizations that obtain ISO 27001 certification prove their dedication to information security while building stakeholder trust.

3. The National Institute of Standards and Technology (NIST) Cybersecurity Framework serves as a voluntary guidance system for organizations to strengthen their cybersecurity practices.

The NIST Cybersecurity Framework serves as a voluntary tool to help organizations advance their cybersecurity methods. The framework provides an adaptable strategy that organizations from various industries can customize to suit their needs. The framework outlines five core functions:

Identify: Understanding the organization's assets, data, and systems.

Protect: Developing safeguards to protect assets and data.

Detect: Implementing measures to detect cybersecurity events.

Respond: Establishing procedures for responding to cybersecurity incidents.

Recover: Developing plans for recovering from cybersecurity incidents.

Many organizations use the NIST Cybersecurity Framework as an essential guide to strengthen their cybersecurity defenses.

4. Industry-Specific Regulations:

SCADA security needs to follow various industry-specific regulations besides baseline standards. Regulatory requirements generally protect data privacy and secure critical infrastructure while ensuring operational safety remains intact. Specific regulations exist for the transportation sector along with distinct regulations for water and healthcare industries.

Every organization needs to identify and comply with all applicable regulations within their industry sector.

5. Geographic Regulations:

Regulatory compliance requirements vary according to geographic location. Businesses operating in multiple countries should understand and comply with the rules of each jurisdiction.

Strategies for Achieving and Maintaining Compliance

Maintaining compliance with SCADA security regulations requires organizations to establish a comprehensive and ongoing process. Key strategies include:

1. Conducting Regular Risk Assessments:

Periodic risk assessments serve as critical tools for identifying system weaknesses and selecting top security measures. Organizations should execute these assessments at a minimum of once per year but must increase the frequency when major changes occur in the SCADA environment. Risk assessments should analyze both industry-specific threats and geographic vulnerabilities that affect an organization.

2. Developing and Implementing Security Policies and Procedures:

Businesses must develop exhaustive security policies and procedures that comprehensively cover all aspects of SCADA security. Security policies must cover various aspects such as access control protocols, vulnerability management strategies, incident response procedures and employee security training programs. Organizations need to create written records of their security policies and provide these documents to appropriate employees followed by regular reviews and updates to match the changing threat landscape and regulatory standards.

3. Implementing Security Controls:

Organizations must establish appropriate security controls based on their completed risk assessments and established security policies. These controls may include:

Network Segmentation: Dividing the SCADA network into smaller isolated segments limits the extent of possible security breaches.

Access Control: Organizations need to adopt powerful authentication and authorization systems to defend sensitive data and systems from unauthorized access.

Vulnerability Management: Vulnerability management requires organizations to perform regular vulnerability scans and apply security patches to address identified weaknesses.

Intrusion Detection and Prevention Systems (IDS/IPS): IDS/IPS systems monitor network traffic patterns to detect malicious activities while simultaneously blocking unauthorized access attempts.

Security Information and Event Management (SIEM): SIEM systems work by collecting security information from numerous sources to enable analysis and management tasks.

Data Loss Prevention (DLP): Through the implementation of DLP solutions organizations can prevent unauthorized transmission of sensitive data outside their network.

4. Employee Training and Awareness:

Companies must implement thorough training programs to teach employees necessary cybersecurity skills. During security training employees must understand how to identify suspicious activities and learn about the importance of safety practices. Regular refresher training sessions help employees stay updated on current security threats and best practices. Simulated phishing attacks and other practical exercises enhance employees' awareness and their security threat response capabilities.

5. Incident Response Planning:

To manage security incidents effectively an organization must develop and test its comprehensive incident response plan. The response plan should outline essential actions together with role allocations and define communication protocols. Personnel should participate in recurring drills and simulations to evaluate the incident response plan's effectiveness.

6. Regular Audits and Compliance Reviews:

The organization should perform routine audits with compliance reviews to verify that security controls operate correctly and conform to regulatory standards. The organization must engage skilled professionals to conduct thorough assessments of all SCADA security program components during audits. Organizations need to evaluate audit findings to identify areas of improvement before updating their security programs accordingly. Independent auditors provide impartial assessments that demonstrate compliance to external entities.

7. Staying Informed on Evolving Regulations and Standards:

The regulatory landscape is constantly evolving. Organizations must monitor updates to regulations and standards and modify their security programs to remain compliant with these changes. Organizations must track regulatory updates while participating in industry conferences and consulting cybersecurity professionals. Members can access updated information by subscribing to pertinent newsletters and becoming part of industry groups.

8. Documentation and Record-Keeping:

Proof of compliance with standards depends on maintaining an exhaustive record of security policies and procedures. Documentation should remain available for audit review and must undergo regular updates to reflect any changes in the security program. Efficient documentation organization facilitates compliance audits and promotes ongoing improvements.

Integrating Compliance with Operational Efficiency

The need to operate efficiently alongside meeting regulatory compliance creates significant challenges. Organizations must design security measures that support operations without causing major disruptions. Strategies for achieving this balance include:

Prioritizing Controls: Organizations need to focus their resources on deploying key security controls derived from risk assessments.

Phased Implementation: Organizations must deploy security controls progressively starting with the areas that hold the highest priority.

Automation: Security procedures automation reduces manual work requirements and heightens operational efficiency.

Collaboration: Our operational teams work together with us to make sure security implementations function in harmony with operations without creating disruptions.

Continuous Monitoring and Improvement: Maintain ongoing observation of security control effectiveness through timely modifications.

Conclusion: Compliance as a Cornerstone of SCADA Security

Building a complete SCADA security framework requires organizations to recognize regulatory compliance as its fundamental building block. Proactive compliance strategies help organizations establish strong security defenses by building stakeholder trust and operational stability while minimizing costly disruptions. Organizations need to persistently monitor and adjust their security practices because threat landscapes and regulatory standards both remain dynamic. The final chapter synthesizes the book's key concepts to deliver a complete guide for building resilient and secure SCADA systems.

Case Study: Compliance Implementation in a Power Generation Facility

The power generation facility generates sufficient electricity to power substantial parts of the major region it serves. This power generation facility operates under the regulatory framework of NERC CIP standards which requires strict cybersecurity measures. These actions represent the facility's efforts to achieve compliance.

Comprehensive Risk Assessment: The facility conducts a thorough risk assessment to identify essential assets and potential threats as well as system vulnerabilities within its SCADA network. The risk evaluation process examines both internal and external dangers including cyberattacks as well as physical security threats and natural disaster scenarios. The evaluation process ranks critical assets by examining their impact on facility operations and their effect on the larger power grid.

Development of Security Policies and Procedures: Based on risk assessment findings the facility develops comprehensive security protocols for access control and vulnerability management along with incident response strategies and employee training programs. Complete documentation of these policies reaches every relevant personnel member. The facility ensures policy updates and evaluations keep pace with new threats to maintain their effectiveness.

Implementation of Security Controls: The facility protects its assets through the implementation of numerous security control measures.

Network Segmentation: Multiple zones segment the SCADA network to separate critical control systems from non-critical components and corporate network access. Organizations implement network segmentation using firewalls and VLANs.

Access Control: Access control measures include strict protocols with multi-factor authentication required for personnel to enter the SCADA system. RBAC establishes a system where users can access only those resources which their roles require.

Vulnerability Management: The organization maintains a consistent vulnerability scanning program which detects vulnerabilities and carries out immediate remediation actions. Patch management systems maintain updated versions of software and firmware across all systems.

Intrusion Detection and Prevention Systems (IDS/IPS): The organization uses IDS/IPS systems to both monitor network traffic for suspicious activity and protect against unauthorized network access.

Security Information and Event Management (SIEM): A SIEM system functions to gather security data from multiple sources which enables continuous analysis and management to achieve complete visibility over the SCADA system's security status.

Physical Security: Facility access to SCADA equipment undergoes strict control through active surveillance systems and access control measures.

Employee Training and Awareness: The facility offers an extensive training program for employees that includes lessons on cybersecurity awareness as well as safe operational practices and response measures for incidents. Staff awareness stays high through ongoing refresher training and simulated phishing tests.

Incident Response Planning: The organization develops a detailed incident response plan which undergoes regular testing through simulations and drills. The plan defines necessary steps for addressing security incidents through specified communication protocols and escalation measures alongside recovery plans.

Regular Audits and Compliance Reviews: The facility regularly completes both internal and external audits to maintain continuous adherence to NERC CIP standards. The audits evaluate security control performance and pinpoint improvement opportunities.

The case study illustrates the extensive process necessary for obtaining and sustaining SCADA security regulation compliance. The facility maintains a strong security posture by proactively managing risks and security measures and implementing continuous monitoring to protect its critical infrastructure and ensure reliable power generation service operations. The knowledge gained from this example serves as applicable guidance for different sectors and organizations responsible for managing critical infrastructure. Organizations that prioritize compliance will establish a solid SCADA security foundation that enhances resilience and reduces cyber threat risks.

Looking Ahead: The Future of SCADA Security and Compliance

Advancements in technology combined with shifting security threats continuously shape the development of the SCADA security field. To remain agile in this dynamic field organizations must commit to learning and adapting continuously while working collaboratively. Future trends include:

Increased Automation: Automation will become essential to strengthen SCADA security while making vulnerability management, incident response, and compliance monitoring more efficient.

AI and Machine Learning: The implementation of AI and machine learning technologies will transform threat detection and response methods to improve the identification and mitigation of advanced attacks.

Blockchain Technology: The exploration and implementation of blockchain technology will improve data integrity and security within SCADA systems.

Enhanced Collaboration: The practice of sharing threat intelligence and best practices will require more cross-industry and cross-border collaboration as it gains importance.

Evolving Regulations: Organizations must remain vigilant and regularly adjust their security programs in response to the continuous updates and refinements of existing regulations.

Organizations that actively respond to current trends and adopt continuous improvement practices will be able to successfully manage SCADA security compliance challenges while maintaining secure and reliable critical infrastructure operations into the future.

The earlier sections established the essential foundation needed to comprehend and put into practice strong SCADA security controls. The final chapter combines essential insights to present an integrated view of creating a strong SCADA system with effective security measures. The final chapter delivers insights into future challenges and opportunities within the dynamic field of industrial cybersecurity.

Synthesizing Key Concepts: A Holistic Approach to SCADA Security

A robust SCADA security framework requires multiple integrated layers that work together to cover various critical aspects.

1. People: Human factors are paramount. The initial defense against security threats starts with building a security-aware culture through thorough training and awareness programs. Employees need to comprehend their responsibilities toward SCADA system protection and develop the skills to detect and report unusual activities. Critical aspects include awareness of social engineering tactics along with safe browsing techniques and strong password creation. Constant refresher training along with simulated attack exercises remain vital to sustain employee alertness.

2. Processes: Security risks require robust processes to manage them effectively. The establishment of clear security policies and procedures must be paired with structured risk assessment methods and the development of a comprehensive incident response plan. All relevant personnel must be informed about security processes which require documentation and periodic revisions. Continuous assessment through audits and compliance reviews maintains operational effectiveness.

3. Technology: SCADA security relies heavily on technological advancements for improvement. Security enhancements for SCADA systems require network segmentation together with access control methods and monitoring instruments that prioritize secure communication. The implementation of next-generation firewalls alongside intrusion detection/prevention systems and both SIEM and EDR solutions boosts the security

posture. Organizations need to customize technology selection and implementation to meet their unique needs and risk profile.

4. Compliance: Organizations need to comply with applicable regulations and standards because they form an essential foundation for maintaining a strong SCADA security posture beyond just satisfying legal obligations. Organizations need to implement crucial security controls to meet compliance standards which results in creating safer systems and building trust among stakeholders. Organizations need to consistently monitor changes in regulations and revise their security programs to match these developments.

5. Continuous Improvement: Securing SCADA systems requires continuous attention and improvement rather than reaching a final state. Organizations need to maintain constant monitoring of their security stance while adapting their protective strategies and strengthening their defenses to keep up with the continuously changing threat landscape. Conducting routine security evaluations and penetration tests alongside post-incident assessments remains crucial to discovering system vulnerabilities and improving overall security strength.

The Practical Framework for Building a Resilient SCADA Environment

The principles discussed above enable organizations to form practical frameworks for SCADA system resilience.

Conduct a Comprehensive Risk Assessment: The SCADA system requires an evaluation of its essential assets alongside possible threats and system weaknesses. Assess risks by ranking them according to their probability and potential consequences.

Develop a Robust Security Policy Framework: Create comprehensive security policies and procedures that address every aspect of SCADA security including access management and vulnerability handling along with incident response measures and staff education.

Implement a Multi-Layered Security Architecture: Create layered cyber defense mechanisms through network segmentation alongside strong authentication methods plus secure communication protocols and advanced monitoring tools.

Establish a Dedicated Security Team: Create a team of experts to take charge of SCADA security management and maintenance. Members of this team need to have specialized knowledge in network security as well as systems administration along with skills in incident response and compliance.

Invest in Employee Training and Awareness: Create and deliver full-scale training courses that teach staff about cyber threats and proper security methods. Performing routine refresher training alongside simulated attacks supports sustained alertness.

Develop and Test an Incident Response Plan: Develop a well-defined incident response plan which specifies the procedures to follow when a security incident arises. Periodic drills and simulations will validate the effectiveness of the response plan and prepare personnel for actual incidents.

Implement a Vulnerability Management Program: Perform regular vulnerability scans and immediately apply necessary security patches to address identified weaknesses.

Establish a Continuous Monitoring and Improvement Program: Perform constant surveillance of the SCADA system to detect suspicious activity while ensuring security policies and procedures reflect both new threats and industry best practices through regular reviews and updates. Keeping up to date with changing regulations and standards is required for this process.

Looking Ahead: Challenges and Opportunities

Future SCADA security developments offer both difficult hurdles to overcome and promising prospects for innovation.

Challenges:

The Increasing Sophistication of Cyber Threats: Organizations must consistently stay ahead because attackers develop new sophisticated techniques constantly.

The Growing Interconnectivity of SCADA Systems: SCADA systems become more vulnerable to attacks as they integrate further with other IT systems which broadens their attack surface.

The Shortage of Skilled Cybersecurity Professionals: Many organizations struggle to locate and keep qualified cybersecurity professionals as a persistent major challenge.

The Complexity of Legacy Systems: SCADA systems frequently depend on outdated equipment and software which presents substantial obstacles to securing and updating them.

The Evolving Regulatory Landscape: Organizations need to monitor updates in regulations and standards continuously and update their security programs to remain compliant.

Opportunities:

Advancements in Security Technologies: Emerging technologies including artificial intelligence (AI), machine learning (ML), and blockchain present substantial opportunities for improving SCADA security systems. Organizations can improve threat detection and response through AI and ML while blockchain technology ensures stronger data integrity and security.

Improved Collaboration and Information Sharing: The cybersecurity community benefits from stronger defenses when members work together to exchange threat intelligence and best practices.

Automation and Orchestration: Security teams can achieve greater efficiency while lessening their workload through the implementation of automation to manage security tasks. Security orchestration tools enable the integration of multiple security technologies to achieve an improved and comprehensive protection strategy.

Focus on Resilience: Organizations must move their security strategy from breach prevention to developing systems that endure attacks and recover effectively. The approach involves putting redundancy mechanisms in place alongside backup solutions and strong recovery strategies.

Conclusion: A Continuous Journey

SCADA security requires constant attention because it represents an ongoing process rather than a final goal. In the dynamic threat environment organizations must maintain constant vigilance while adapting and committing to perpetual improvement. Organizations achieve resilient and secure SCADA environments which can resist modern cyber challenges by implementing a holistic approach that combines people management, process optimization, technological applications, and compliance standards. Organizations need to maintain a proactive approach and dedicate resources to effective security measures while building a strong organization-wide security culture. Organizations must adapt to new threats, apply technological advancements, and engage in effective collaboration to share knowledge and best practices to ensure the future of SCADA security. The protection of our world's essential infrastructure requires constant joint efforts by everyone involved.

Chapter 10: Emerging technologies and trends of the future of SCADA security

The previous chapters showed how SCADA security operates on multiple levels which requires an all-encompassing strategy that integrates people, processes, technology and compliance standards. The cybersecurity landscape demonstrates continuous change as it evolves over time. This chapter provides an analysis of new technologies and trends which will determine the future trajectory of SCADA security by presenting both the benefits they offer and the challenges they introduce.

The Ever-Evolving Threat Landscape

The security challenges that SCADA systems face are evolving to become more sophisticated and complex. Attackers utilize sophisticated artificial intelligence (AI) and machine learning (ML) methods to create stealthier and more efficient attacks. The need for ongoing security strategy updates along with emerging technology adoption will ensure sustained robust security protection. Several primary trends are determining the future threat landscape.

Increased Automation of Attacks: Attackers today frequently deploy automated tools and techniques for large-scale attacks. The advancement of automated attacks raises the difficulty level for manual threat detection and response.

Sophisticated Use of AI and ML by Attackers: Malware development and security control bypass along with personalized phishing attacks are becoming more effective thanks to attackers using AI and ML technologies. Organizations must implement sophisticated threat detection and response techniques to address these challenges.

Exploitation of IoT Devices: The rapid increase of IoT devices in industrial settings creates more opportunities for attackers to target SCADA systems. The majority of IoT devices have insufficient security measures that leave them open to attacks.

Rise of Advanced Persistent Threats (APTs): Advanced Persistent Threats (APTs) represent a severe risk to SCADA security because they combine stealth with sustained attacks against specific targets. These attacks demand complex detection systems and advanced response capabilities.

Supply Chain Attacks: If attackers gain control over SCADA vendors' supply chains they can access multiple systems through backdoors. A complete review of vendors and enhanced supply chain protection measures must be implemented.

Emerging Technologies Shaping SCADA Security

Emerging technologies possess great potential to boost SCADA security measures.

1. Artificial Intelligence (AI) and Machine Learning (ML):

AI and ML technologies transform cybersecurity operations by enhancing threat detection capabilities while improving response mechanisms. These technologies process large data sets to detect malicious activity patterns which help to issue early warnings of prospective attacks. Specific applications include:

Anomaly Detection: Through analysis of system behavior AI and ML algorithms detect abnormal patterns which help flag potential security threats.

Predictive Threat Modeling: The use of historical data combined with emerging trends allows these technologies to forecast potential security threats which enables organizations to implement proactive protection strategies.

Automated Incident Response: Incident response tasks such as system isolation and malicious traffic blocking can be automated by AI and ML technologies.

Malware Analysis: AI and ML technologies help analyze malware samples while discovering their characteristics and creating defense strategies.

Successful SCADA security through AI and ML demands extensive funding for data infrastructure as well as algorithm development and expert personnel.

2. Blockchain Technology:

SCADA systems stand to benefit from blockchain technology through improved data integrity and security features. System events achieve tamper-proof status through blockchain technology because of its decentralized and immutable nature which boosts trust and transparency. Potential applications include:

Secure Data Logging: Blockchain ensures SCADA system events remain secure and untampered while enhancing audit capabilities and supporting incident response operations.

Supply Chain Security: Blockchain technology strengthens supply chain security through its transparent verification process which confirms the origin and authenticity of SCADA components.

Secure Device Management: SCADA devices can be securely managed and authenticated through blockchain technology which blocks unauthorized access while maintaining device integrity.

Blockchain technology has only begun to be utilized in SCADA security systems yet offers substantial improvements in trust and security capabilities.

3. Zero Trust Security:

Under the Zero Trust security model every user or device must undergo verification before being granted access as no entity receives default trust based on location or network position. Resources require user and device identity verification at every access attempt in this model. The main elements of Zero Trust security in SCADA environments consist of:

Micro segmentation: Create extremely small, isolated segments within the SCADA network to restrict breach impacts.

Continuous Authentication: Systems must conduct ongoing identity checks of users and devices even after their initial log-in process.

Least Privilege Access: Users should receive only the access levels needed to perform their specific duties.

Data Encryption: The protection of data confidentiality and integrity requires encryption of data during movement and when stored.

Implementing Zero Trust requires organizations to undergo a substantial transformation in security architecture and thinking while providing stronger defenses against advanced cyber threats.

4. Secure Access Service Edge (SASE):

Secure Access Service Edge (SASE) combines secure web gateways with VPNs and cloud access security brokers (CASBs) to create an integrated cloud-based security service. This method streamlines remote access security management while boosting protection levels for SCADA systems spread across multiple locations. Key benefits include:

Simplified Management: Using a cloud-based service to integrate security functions allows organizations to simplify administrative processes and minimize operational complexity.

Improved Performance: Real-time SCADA systems benefit from cloud-based delivery because it increases performance while reducing latency.

Enhanced Security: SASE solutions offer enhanced security through features like advanced threat protection capabilities alongside data loss prevention (DLP) systems.

Scalability and Flexibility: The scalable nature of cloud-based solutions enables organizations to adjust quickly as their requirements evolve.

5. Quantum-Resistant Cryptography:

The progression of quantum computing technology threatens the security of current encryption algorithms. Quantum-resistant cryptography provides protection against quantum computer attacks to ensure secure data protection over extended periods. Preparing for this shift requires organizations to:

Research and Evaluate Algorithms: Monitor progress in creating and standardizing cryptographic algorithms that can resist quantum attacks.

Plan for Migration: Create a strategic approach to transition to quantum-resistant cryptographic systems when required.

Collaborate with Industry: Engage with industry partners and standards bodies to facilitate seamless changes.

Challenges in Adopting Emerging Technologies

The full adoption of emerging technologies for SCADA security faces numerous obstacles despite their potential.

Cost and Complexity: The deployment of these technologies demands substantial investments in infrastructure, software, and skilled personnel which makes the process both costly and complex.

Integration Issues: The process of integrating new technologies alongside legacy systems presents challenges that may necessitate substantial system modifications or complete replacements.

Skills Gap: The effectiveness of implementing these technologies is restricted by the limited availability of skilled cybersecurity professionals who understand emerging technologies.

Data Management: Organizations must invest heavily in data infrastructure and management capabilities to utilize AI and ML effectively.

Regulatory Uncertainty: Organizations face uncertainty because the regulations governing these technologies remain in development.

Conclusion: A Continuous Journey of Adaptation

Organizations must learn to adapt to changing threats and use new technologies to ensure SCADA security's future success. Organizations face substantial challenges but stand to gain considerable benefits. Organizations that employ advanced security technologies and promote security awareness while adopting proactive risk management strategies can establish SCADA environments that endure modern cyber threats. Success in industrial cybersecurity depends on ongoing education combined with team efforts and dedication to maintaining a leading edge in this dynamic field. Enhanced SCADA security requires an ongoing process that involves maintaining vigilance and adapting to new threats while committing to perpetual improvement efforts.

Chapter 11: Establishing a Culture of Security through the Balanced Integration of People, Processes and Technology

This book presents diverse SCADA security topics and underlines the necessity for a comprehensive defense strategy that integrates human elements, procedural guidelines, and technological tools. The most successful security strategy combines multiple elements into a unified system which stands on the essential groundwork of security culture. This chapter examines how to develop a security-aware organizational culture for entities that manage SCADA systems by demonstrating how people and processes work together with technology to create effective cybersecurity solutions.

Beyond Technology: The Human Element in SCADA Security

SCADA security system depends equally on technological solutions and the capabilities of the personnel who manage them. Organizations need to build a strong security culture where all members share responsibility for security that defines the organization's core values. The culture extends beyond technical skills to include organizational attitudes and behaviors which all contribute to a shared understanding of cybersecurity's critical importance. A robust security culture incorporates several vital elements.

Leadership Commitment: Leadership needs to actively promote security efforts by investing in protective measures while allocating adequate resources and upholding accountability for security policy adherence. The leadership commitment establishes security as a primary organizational focus through its influence throughout the organization.

Shared Responsibility: The responsibility for security extends beyond IT staff and security personnel. Every organizational member must participate in maintaining the company's security posture regardless of their specific role. Organizations must build a culture where all individuals recognize their specific responsibilities for SCADA system protection.

Proactive Security Mindset: Proactive security approaches focus on threat anticipation and prevention instead of only responding to security incidents. An essential part of maintaining security readiness includes standard training on security awareness and threat modeling exercises along with adopting the latest security technologies and practices.

Open Communication and Collaboration: Communication channels that remain open allow teams to report security incidents promptly while supporting joint efforts between various teams and departments. Organizations can build collective responsibility through consistent security awareness campaigns, internal newsletters and open forums.

Continuous Learning and Improvement: The cybersecurity landscape is constantly evolving. Organizations which build a culture of ongoing learning and enhancement maintain their security advantage over new threats through adaptive security strategy development. Protection of the threat landscape depends on consistent training efforts as well as active participation in industry events with ongoing threat monitoring.

Accountability and Consequences: Organizations must establish explicit expectations and repercussions to handle security breaches effectively. Security policies and procedures gain importance through individual understanding of their necessity. Organizations need to establish clear disciplinary procedures to handle security infractions.

Aligning People, Processes, and Technology

A strong SCADA security program combines people, processes, and technology in a cohesive manner. Effective interaction between each element is essential to achieve comprehensive protection because every element has a critical role.

People: Employees who receive proper training and stay alert serve as the initial defense against social engineering attacks along with phishing scams and insider threats. The effectiveness of security protocols relies on personnel maintaining constant vigilance to prevent system breaches.

Processes: Clearly articulated processes lead to consistent and effective implementation of security measures. Security measures require setting up strong risk evaluation systems alongside detailed emergency response strategies and routine security checks. These processes establish an essential structure for both risk management and timely incident response.

Technology: The necessary tools and infrastructure to implement successful security controls are provided by technology. Technology solutions encompass network segmentation along with access control mechanisms and intrusion detection and prevention systems as well as security information and event management (SIEM) systems and data loss prevention (DLP) tools. Technology alone falls short if organizations do not establish a strong security culture alongside clear processes.

Fostering a Culture of Security: Practical Strategies

Developing a robust security culture demands multiple strategies that work together.

Leadership Buy-in: Secure top-level management support for cybersecurity initiatives. A robust security program requires the allocation of adequate financial resources as well as personnel and assets.

Comprehensive Training Programs: Implement extensive training programs for SCADA security that cover social engineering awareness and phishing prevention as well as secure browsing practices and incident response procedures. Design training programs that cater to the specific roles and responsibilities of each organizational position.

Regular Security Awareness Campaigns: Implement frequent security awareness initiatives to strengthen essential principles and update employees about new security threats. To achieve maximum engagement, use various communication channels including emails newsletters, posters and interactive workshops.

Simulated Phishing Exercises: Perform routine simulated phishing tests to evaluate employee awareness levels while strengthening their training. This exercise creates a lifelike situation for employees to develop their skills in detecting and reporting suspicious emails.

Incentivize Secure Behavior: Identify and reward staff members who actively engage in secure behavior practices. Incentives for reporting suspicious activities alongside participation in training programs and proposing security enhancements represent this approach.

Establish Clear Reporting Mechanisms: Set up straightforward and available channels through which employees can report security incidents. Employees need to know they can report suspicious activities without worrying about negative consequences. Building trust along with maintaining open communication is essential.

Regular Security Audits and Reviews: Perform routine security audits and evaluations to evaluate control effectiveness and pinpoint improvement opportunities. This process generates useful feedback which ensures that the security program stays both relevant and effective.

Continuous Monitoring and Improvement: Maintain constant surveillance of the SCADA system to detect suspicious activities while routinely revising security policies to address new threats and incorporate best practices. Through this iterative approach, the security program stays updated to counteract the changing threat environment.

Collaboration and Information Sharing: Organizational teams and departments should work together internally and establish information-sharing networks with external industry partners. Through this approach organizations can exchange threat intelligence and best practices to boost collective security.

Measuring the Effectiveness of Security Culture

While measuring the effectiveness of security culture presents challenges it remains essential for both demonstrating its impact and finding areas that need improvement. Key metrics include:

Number of Security Incidents: The effectiveness of security measures can be evaluated by monitoring changes in security incident frequency over time. The reduction in security incidents demonstrates the beneficial outcomes of security measures.

Time to Detect and Respond to Incidents: The duration of incident detection and response times serves as an indicator of security program effectiveness. When response times shrink organizations demonstrate stronger security defenses.

Employee Awareness and Training Completion Rates: The evaluation of awareness initiatives effectiveness depends on tracking employee attendance in training programs and their grasp of essential security concepts.

Number of Security Policies and Procedures Violations: The analysis of security violations helps expose shortcomings in security awareness and training programs.

Employee Feedback and Surveys: Employee surveys and focus group discussions provide essential insights on security initiative effectiveness and help pinpoint improvement areas.

Case Study: Strengthening Security Culture in Water Treatment Operations

The water treatment facility launched a broad program designed to build and maintain a security-focused culture. This involved:

Executive Sponsorship: The CEO led the security initiative by underlining its importance and directing resources towards it.

Targeted Training: Different roles received customized training programs that focused on their unique security concerns such as those relevant to SCADA operators, IT staff, and administrative personnel.

Gamified Security Awareness: The use of interactive online modules alongside simulated phishing exercises improved both the engagement level and effectiveness of the training.

Open Communication Channels: An anonymous reporting system coupled with regular newsletters and internal meetings supported open communication as well as teamwork.

Reward and Recognition: The organization provided recognition and rewards for employees who detected and reported security vulnerabilities.

Continuous Monitoring and Improvement: The organization performed consistent security audits and post-incident reviews which assessed security measures and pinpointed improvement areas.

The initiative produced better security results through fewer security incidents and heightened employee awareness which enhanced collective security responsibility.

Conclusion: Security Culture as a Foundation for Resilience

Establishing a strong security culture demands persistent work and resources since it extends beyond a single project to become a continual process. Organizations that build a culture of shared security responsibility greatly boost the success rate of their SCADA security programs. The combined effectiveness of human resources and technological systems alongside structured processes establishes a strong and secure SCADA environment which successfully withstands the constantly changing threat landscape. The foundation of a truly secure SCADA system rests on a strong security culture that integrates trust with collaborative efforts and ongoing improvement commitments. Securing critical infrastructure and maintaining essential service reliability depends fundamentally on a human-centric approach.

Chapter 12: The process of updating SCADA systems requires finding a balance between implementing robust security measures and preserving operational effectiveness.

The modernization of SCADA systems remains essential to improve security measures while ensuring operational efficiency amid today's intricate networked environment. Outdated SCADA systems lack built-in security features which creates major vulnerabilities to cyber threats. This chapter examines both the difficulties and possibilities in SCADA system modernization while presenting methods to maintain operational efficiency alongside security improvements.

Challenges in Modernizing SCADA Systems

Modernizing SCADA systems presents several significant challenges:

Legacy System Dependency: Numerous organizations depend on legacy SCADA systems which present major challenges due to their high replacement or upgrade costs. Most SCADA systems do not come with inherent security features, and they cannot work with modern security technologies. The complexity of the system combined with its integration into current infrastructure creates challenging upgrading requirements.

Integration Complexity: Combining new technological solutions with established legacy systems presents significant challenges which take considerable time to overcome. Successful integration demands meticulous planning alongside testing and validation procedures which help maintain compatibility and preserve operational continuity. The ability of multiple systems and protocols to operate together presents a major challenge.

Cost Considerations: The process of upgrading SCADA systems involves substantial costs due to the need for fresh hardware and software purchases as well as training and additional professional services. Organizations need to evaluate both the financial implications and potential advantages of system modernization versus the dangers involved with continuing to use outdated systems. To convince stakeholders about the expenditure it is essential to provide them with a transparent demonstration of return on investment (ROI).

Operational Disruptions: When organizations upgrade or replace SCADA systems they face the risk of temporary operational interruptions. Properly scheduled downtime combined with thorough testing procedures are essential for reducing operational disruptions and maintaining continuous business operations. The process necessitates collaboration between IT specialists and operational staff.

Skills Gap: Modernization efforts may face obstacles due to a lack of trained professionals who understand both SCADA systems and cybersecurity principles. The successful modernization of systems demands both staff training programs and the hiring of skilled new employees.

Strategies for Modernizing SCADA Systems

Modernization strategies require a balance between improving security measures and sustaining operational performance levels. Key strategies include:

Phased Approach: Organizations can modernize their SCADA systems step by step through a phased approach instead of complete system replacement. Through this method organizations can minimize operational disruption while ensuring each stage of modernization undergoes thorough testing and validation. Organizations commonly use the strategy of upgrading critical systems before others.

Prioritization: Begin SCADA system modernization by upgrading its most critical and vulnerable components. The modernization process starts by targeting the highest security risks to ensure they get addressed first. A risk assessment enables organizations to identify systems that demand urgent attention.

Virtualization and Cloud Computing: The process of virtualizing SCADA components leads to enhancements in scalability while also providing flexibility and improved security features. Cloud computing delivers extra advantages including cost savings in infrastructure and improved disaster recovery options. Security considerations must be carefully evaluated when utilizing cloud environments.

Network Segmentation and Access Control: Enhancing security requires the implementation of strong network segmentation and access control measures. These measures contain breach damage and block unauthorized system access. The principle of least privilege (PoLP) makes sure users receive just the access they need.

Improved Authentication and Authorization: Enhanced security results from modern authentication mechanisms like multi-factor authentication (MFA) and role-based access control (RBAC). MFA enhances security by providing an extra protective barrier which complicates unauthorized access attempts by attackers.

Secure Communication Protocols: The transition to more secure communication protocols such as OPC UA improves data confidentiality and integrity. Modbus and other outdated protocols lack inherent security mechanisms and need either replacement or additional security measures.

Intrusion Detection and Prevention Systems (IDS/IPS): Implementing IDS/IPS solutions strengthens organizations' ability to detect and respond to threats. These systems keep track of network traffic patterns to detect malicious activities and alert users to impending attacks.

Security Information and Event Management (SIEM): SIEM systems create a centralized system which enables organizations to gather and evaluate security information from multiple sources while managing security operations. Organizations gain enhanced visibility to their SCADA security system status while streamlining their incident response process.

Data Loss Prevention (DLP): DLP solutions stop sensitive information from leaving the network without proper authorization while safeguarding critical operational data against theft and unauthorized access.

Regular Security Audits and Penetration Testing: Performing consistent security audits and penetration testing remains essential to discover system weaknesses and evaluate security measures' efficiency. Qualified professionals need to perform assessments which encompass every element of the SCADA system.

Balancing Security Enhancements and Operational Needs

Modernization initiatives require careful consideration to enhance security measures while sustaining operational efficiency levels. Strategies for achieving this balance include:

Incremental Upgrades: Apply system upgrades over multiple stages to limit interruptions in current operations.

Thorough Testing and Validation: It is essential to perform rigorous testing and validation of new systems and software before deployment to prevent operational problems.

Employee Training: A complete training program for employees regarding new system operations and security protocols plays a critical role in achieving seamless transitions and reducing mistakes.

Collaboration between IT and Operations: The operational efficiency of systems must remain intact, which requires close collaboration between IT and operational teams during security enhancement processes. A mutual understanding of security and operational requirements must be supported by transparent communication channels.

Realistic Expectations: The modernization process requires stakeholders to maintain realistic expectations. Modernization demands consistent effort through its complex and iterative nature which requires patience.

Case Study: Modernizing the Water Distribution SCADA System

A large water distribution company took the decision to update its outdated SCADA system. The company implemented a phased modernization strategy by addressing the most essential system components initially. The modernization included:

Network Segmentation: The SCADA network underwent segmentation into different zones which served to separate critical control systems from other components and the corporate network. The implementation of firewalls and VLANs achieved the required network segmentation.

Multi-factor Authentication (MFA): Implementing multi-factor authentication for SCADA system access strengthened security measures and prevented unauthorized access.

OPC UA Migration: By switching to OPC UA from outdated communication protocols the company managed to strengthen data confidentiality and integrity.

Intrusion Detection System (IDS): The organization implemented an intrusion detection system to monitor network traffic for signs of malicious activity while alerting to potential attacks early.

Security Information and Event Management (SIEM): The implementation of a SIEM system enabled the collection and analysis of security data from multiple sources which enhanced the visibility of the SCADA system's security posture.

Employee Training: Employees received thorough instruction about the new system and security procedures through comprehensive training. This included hands-on training and simulated scenarios.

The modernization process occurred through multiple stages which helped reduce interruptions to existing operations. The firm meticulously scheduled downtime while performing extensive testing before launching new system components. Modernization efforts resulted in a SCADA system that operates more securely and efficiently while being better prepared to handle contemporary cyber threats.

Emerging Technologies and Future Trends

Several emerging technologies show great potential to boost SCADA modernization initiatives.

Artificial Intelligence (AI) and Machine Learning (ML): AI and ML capabilities help to enhance threat detection systems while automating incident response protocols and improving operational efficiency. These technologies enable the analysis of massive data sets to detect patterns that suggest malicious activity and forecast possible threats.

Blockchain Technology: Blockchain technology strengthens data security and integrity through its ability to create immutable records of system events. This technology proves especially beneficial for performing audits and meeting compliance requirements.

Internet of Things (IoT) Security: The integration of additional IoT devices into SCADA systems necessitates stronger security measures to protect these devices. Secure communication protocols, strong authentication methods, and routine firmware updates form vital components of IoT security.

Edge Computing: Real-time SCADA systems require reduced latency and enhanced responsiveness which edge computing delivers by processing data near its origin point. However, securing edge devices is crucial.

Quantum-Resistant Cryptography: Organizations need to migrate towards quantum-resistant cryptography because advancing quantum computing technology threatens future data security.

Conclusion: A Continuous Process of Modernization

SCADA systems modernization requires constant investment and effort because it is not a single event but an ongoing process. The implementation of a step-by-step plan combined with a focus on essential system elements and the application of new technologies enables organizations to improve both the protection and functionality of their SCADA systems. Successful modernization requires close collaboration between IT and operational teams along with thorough testing and validation and comprehensive employee training. Maintaining a resilient SCADA infrastructure requires organizations to commit to ongoing improvement efforts and adapt to the changing threat landscape because cyber threats are becoming more sophisticated. Modernization requires a continuous proactive strategy to maintain the security and efficiency of SCADA systems for future years.

Chapter 13: Our roadmap toward a resilient future hinge on a holistic methodology for SCADA cybersecurity.

In this book we examined SCADA security's complex nature by studying the technological, procedural, and human aspects which build strong cyber defense mechanisms. The concluding chapter integrates the main concepts to present an integrated view on creating a future-ready SCADA system that combines both resilience and security. The text highlights how continuous improvement together with adaptive strategies and collaborative efforts are essential for managing the dynamic world of industrial cybersecurity.

SCADA security requires a systems approach to understanding how different security elements are interconnected.

SCADA security functions as an integrated system that unites people with processes and technology to create a harmonious security environment. Security weaknesses arise when various security components operate in isolation from one another. A holistic systems-thinking methodology acknowledges the interdependence between these components while emphasizing their smooth integration.

Comprehensive training and awareness programs generate a powerful security culture which stands as the foundation for success. It is crucial that employees comprehend their responsibilities toward the SCADA security system and receive the authority to recognize and communicate any suspicious activities. The program covers technical staff as well as operational personnel while extending to management teams and external contractors. Maintaining vigilance and creating shared responsibility demands regular training while executing simulated attacks in combination with open communication channels.

Processes: Effective management of security risks requires clearly established operational processes. The strategy requires building strong risk assessment methods while creating complete incident response strategies and performing consistent security audits and compliance evaluations. These processes establish a structure for proactive risk management and swift incident response while promoting ongoing improvement efforts. Security measures require documentation to ensure both transparency and consistent application during audits.

Technology: Effective security controls require the tools and infrastructure which technology supplies. Organizations employ network segmentation alongside access control systems and IDS/IPS for threat management while implementing SIEM systems and DLP tools together with advanced threat detection technologies. Technology cannot achieve comprehensive security without the support of both a strong security culture and clearly defined processes. Organizations need to customize their technology selection and deployment process to meet their unique needs and risk levels while considering budget limitations, current infrastructure capabilities, and operational requirements.

Building Resilience: Beyond Prevention to Mitigation and Recovery

A truly resilient SCADA system defends against attacks and maintains functionality while also quickly recovering from incidents. Resilience requires a multi-pronged approach:

Redundancy and Failover Mechanisms: Implementing redundant systems along with failover mechanisms allows critical operations to remain functional despite individual component failures or security breaches. The strategy comprises redundant network infrastructure solutions alongside backup power systems and duplicate SCADA servers.

Robust Backup and Recovery Plans: To minimize downtime during security incidents organizations must establish comprehensive recovery plans while keeping critical data backed up on a regular basis. Organizations must perform regular tests of these plans to verify they function properly.

Incident Response Planning: Organizations need a clear incident response plan to effectively manage cyber incident responses and recovery procedures. The response plan must detail assigned roles and responsibilities along with communication protocols and procedures for containment, eradication, and recovery. The effectiveness of the plan depends on routine drills and simulations.

Continuous Monitoring and Threat Intelligence: Early detection of potential threats becomes possible when organizations implement continuous SCADA system monitoring together with threat intelligence feeds. Through proactive actions organizations can quickly respond to incidents and reduce their negative effects.

Supply Chain Security: SCADA systems remain vulnerable to attackers through compromised vendors because supply chain security is essential to prevent such backdoor access. Organizations must perform exhaustive vendor evaluations while maintaining secure procurement methods and conduct regular audits of vendor security measures.

The Role of Collaboration and Information Sharing

The security of SCISA systems improves when organizations engage in collaborative efforts and exchange information. Organizations can benefit significantly from:

Industry Information Sharing and Analysis Centers (ISACs): Through ISAC participation organizations gain access to threat intelligence and sector-specific best practices. The industry's security posture becomes stronger through collective intelligence.

Government Agencies and Cybersecurity Organizations: Working together with government agencies and cybersecurity organizations delivers access to important threat intelligence and essential resources. Through collaboration entities achieve better situational awareness which leads to improved response capabilities.

Public-Private Partnerships: Public-private partnerships enable government agencies to work together with industry organizations and cybersecurity firms to promote coordinated resource sharing and information exchange.

Emerging Technologies and Future Trends

A range of innovative technologies holds great promise for strengthening SCADA security measures.

Artificial Intelligence (AI) and Machine Learning (ML): By applying AI and ML organizations can achieve better threat detection capabilities while automating incident responses and enhancing operational efficiency.

Blockchain Technology: Blockchain technology strengthens security by maintaining data integrity through an unalterable archive of system activities.

Quantum-Resistant Cryptography: Organizations need to adopt quantum-resistant cryptographic algorithms to protect sensitive information as quantum computing technology continues to develop.

Secure Access Service Edge (SASE): The Secure Access Service Edge (SASE) model combines network security features with cloud delivery to streamline remote access management.

Zero Trust Architecture: Zero Trust architecture operates without assuming trust in any entity and demands perpetual authentication of both users and devices.

To successfully implement these technologies, organizations must allocate funds for infrastructure development and skills training while embracing new approaches.

A Forward-Looking Perspective: The Continuous Journey of SCADA Security

Securing SCADA systems requires constant attention and evolution rather than reaching a final endpoint. The dynamic nature of security threats requires constant monitoring along with adaptive strategies and a dedication to continuous enhancement. Organizations need to adopt a comprehensive framework which integrates people, processes, and technology together with compliance to establish a robust security culture that impacts every level of the organization.

Creating a resilient SCADA environment needs organizations to adopt a proactive approach while investing in strong security measures and committing to collaborative information exchange. Organizations can develop strong defenses against cyberattacks and maintain operational security for critical infrastructure when they implement these guiding principles.

Key Takeaways and Recommendations

This book presents multiple essential lessons and suggestions for improving SCADA security systems.

Prioritize a Strong Security Culture: Develop an organizational culture that emphasizes shared security responsibility and positions security as a foundational value which allows employees to enhance the organization's security posture. The approach entails complete training programs alongside open lines of communication and a culture that focuses on continual advancement.

Implement a Multi-Layered Security Approach: Develop a defense system that combines technology tools, business procedures and human resources to build strong security protection. Organizations need to implement network segmentation together with access control systems alongside intrusion detection and prevention measures while maintaining regular vulnerability management and establishing strong incident response plans.

Embrace a Proactive Approach: Prioritize threat anticipation and prevention as your key strategy instead of just responding to security incidents. Organizations should utilize threat intelligence data to perform routine security evaluations and then apply security measures in a proactive manner.

Invest in Modernization: Maintain SCADA systems security by continually updating their infrastructure to resolve vulnerabilities and integrate new technologies. Phased implementation makes system upgrades manageable while reducing operational disruptions.

Ensure Compliance: Follow all current regulations and standards while making sure security protocols comply with legal and industry requirements. Maintaining compliance requires regular performance of audits and reviews.

Foster Collaboration: Engage in industry information-sharing initiatives and work together with other organizations to exchange threat intelligence and best practices.

Conclusion: Securing a Critical Future

The protection of SCADA systems holds vital importance because threats to these systems can affect both single organizations and larger aspects such as social health, economic stability, and national security. Advanced cyber threats combined with growing system interconnectivity demand continuous proactive security measures. Organizations that adopt the book's comprehensive strategies which merge people, processes, and technology with a solid culture of security will develop robust SCADA environments that endure modern cyber threats. Enhancing SCADA security remains a perpetual obligation that demands consistent vigilance and adaptation while requiring collective dedication to safeguard critical infrastructure. Our interconnected world's future relies on this principle.

Epilogue: A Continuous Vigil

The exploration of SCADA security concludes with the reminder that achieving enhanced protection requires an ongoing process rather than reaching a destination. The dynamic nature of security threats requires constant alertness together with adaptability and an unwavering dedication to improving processes. Cyberattacks become more sophisticated over time which requires security strategies to remain proactive and adaptable.

Modern SCADA systems enable enhanced efficiency and control but introduce substantial security challenges due to their interconnected nature. A single system component breach can rapidly propagate through the network and cause extensive operational disruption. Due to the interconnected nature of systems administrators need to implement comprehensive security approaches that integrate technology safeguards with human factors and cultural practices related to cybersecurity.

The human factor remains a critical vulnerability. Human mistakes and negligence along with unawareness can make even the strongest technological defenses useless. Organizations must invest equally in employee training programs and a strong security culture along with open communication channels to match the effectiveness of advanced security technologies.

As we move forward, emerging technologies present both beneficial opportunities and challenging obstacles. The combination of artificial intelligence, machine learning, and blockchain technology offers vast opportunities to boost threat detection capabilities while enhancing incident response effectiveness and maintaining data integrity. Successful deployment of advanced technologies demands substantial infrastructure investment and skill-building while requiring organizations to embrace new methods.

Organizations must adapt their security programs in response to the continuous changes in the regulatory environment to maintain proper compliance. An effective security strategy relies on compliance as a fundamental element beyond its legal obligations. Following proper standards and regulations enables organizations to implement security measures that fortify their defenses against cyber threats.

The security of SCADA systems depends on everyone working together to maintain continuous improvement through collaboration and information sharing. It is essential for organizations to engage in information-sharing activities within their industry while partnering with cybersecurity professionals and keeping up to date with new threats and best practices. The effective protection of modern world infrastructure needs constant collective efforts from multiple parties. Continuous vigilance and relentless adaptation must underpin our unwavering commitment. The hidden protectors of our globally connected systems must receive equivalent recognition and support.

Glossary of Terms: Beyond the Firewall

This glossary defines key terms used throughout Beyond the Firewall: Strengthening SCADA security measures during this era of rising cyber threats.

Access Control: Access control involves limiting computer system and network resource accessibility through the application of the least privilege principle. The process requires verifying user identity through authentication and determining allowed user actions through authorization.

Advanced Persistent Threat (APT): A sophisticated long-duration cyberattack often executed by state-sponsored entities or expert cybercriminals represents an advanced persistent threat. Advanced Persistent Threats (APTs) maintain their presence through stealthy operations while focusing on clearly defined objectives.

Anomaly Detection: Anomaly Detection refers to the identification of atypical patterns or behavior changes in computer systems and networks which usually suggest a security incident. This often leverages machine learning algorithms.

Authentication: The verification procedure that confirms whether a user or device has the right to access a computer system or network resource. Methods include passwords, multi-factor authentication, and biometrics.

Authorization: Authorization determines which actions users and devices can perform following successful authentication.

The assignment of permissions typically revolves around user roles.

Backup: Data backups consist of separate data copies that allow for system recovery when data gets lost or when a system breakdown occurs. Regular backups are crucial for disaster recovery.

Black Energy: The sophisticated malware Black Energy launched attacks on Ukrainian power grids to show that critical infrastructure can face widespread disruption.

Blockchain Technology: Blockchain technology serves as a decentralized ledger system which maintains data integrity while also improving security measures. SCADA systems could benefit from secure data logging and supply chain management applications.

Botnet: A collection of hijacked computers functions under the remote command of a malicious actor. Attackers use networks of compromised computers known as botnets to execute distributed denial-of-service (DDoS) attacks.

Cloud Computing: The provision of computer system resources such as data storage and computing power occurs on-demand without requiring direct management intervention from users. SCADA scalability and resilience can improve with this approach but demands thorough security planning.

Compliance: Following all applicable cybersecurity regulations and standards as well as legal requirements remains essential. Maintaining compliance standards plays a vital role in preventing legal consequences while building stakeholder confidence.

Critical Infrastructure: Society depends on essential systems and assets like power grids, water treatment plants, transportation networks, and communication systems for its operations. SCADA systems serve as essential parts for critical infrastructure.

Cybersecurity: Cybersecurity protects computer systems and networks alongside their data against unauthorized usage and alterations as well as against disclosure and destruction.

Data Loss Prevention (DLP): Data Loss Prevention (DLP) utilizes security tools to stop sensitive information from leaving organizational control through network monitoring and data encryption.

Denial-of-Service (DoS) Attack: This attack seeks to block access to network resources for legitimate users. The attack works by overwhelming the target with too much traffic.

Distributed Denial-of-Service (DDoS) Attack: A DoS attack that uses multiple compromised systems as launch points (often through a botnet) presents greater challenges for mitigation.

Dragonfly: A complex APT campaign operated against energy facilities throughout the United States and Europe.

Encryption: Encryption involves transforming data into a scrambled form which safeguards its confidential nature. Decryption reverses this process.

Endpoint Detection and Response (EDR): Endpoint Protection software operates on individual devices to identify and counteract malware and other cybersecurity risks.

Firewall: This network security device regulates both incoming and outgoing network traffic through the application of established security protocols.

Human-Machine Interface (HMI): The Human-Machine Interface (HMI) allows users to interact with SCADA systems through data visualization and process control capabilities.

Industrial Control System (ICS): The Industrial Control System (ICS) monitors and manages industrial equipment operations and process controls. SCADA is a type of ICS.

Incident Response: Incident Response encompasses preparation for cybersecurity incidents alongside their detection, analysis, containment, eradication, recovery and subsequent learning process.

Intrusion Detection System (IDS): The Intrusion Detection System (IDS) analyzes network traffic to identify malicious activities while notifying administrators about possible security breaches.

Intrusion Prevention System (IPS): The Intrusion Prevention System (IPS) functions to stop malicious network traffic from entering the network and causing intrusions.

Internet of Things (IoT): The Internet of Things (IoT) connects physical objects known as "things" through embedded electronics along with software components and network connectivity which allows these objects to sense and transfer data. SCADA environments that use IoT devices experience both beneficial opportunities and significant security challenges.

Jump Server: As an intermediary point for network access the secure server connects users to internal systems while enhancing security by reducing direct system exposure.

Least Privilege (PoLP): The least privilege principle ensures users receive only essential access required for their work tasks to reduce risks from compromised accounts.

Malware: Software that performs malicious actions which damage systems or provide unauthorized access to computer resources. This includes viruses, worms, trojans, and ransomware.

Multi-Factor Authentication (MFA): Multi-Factor Authentication (MFA) enhances security by requiring users to provide multiple verification methods to validate their identity beyond standard password systems.

National Institute of Standards and Technology (NIST): The National Institute of Standards and Technology (NIST) functions as a U.S. government agency that creates and supports technology standards while focusing on cybersecurity solutions. The NIST Cybersecurity Framework is widely adopted.

Network Access Control (NAC): This system manages network access by evaluating both the identity and security status of devices to allow only authorized secure devices to connect.

Network Segmentation: Network segmentation involves breaking down a network into separate smaller sections to minimize the consequences of security breaches.

North American Electric Reliability Corporation (NERC): The North American Electric Reliability Corporation functions as a non-profit organization that maintains North America's bulk power system reliability. The Critical Infrastructure Protection standards from NERC focus specifically on protecting the electric grid from cybersecurity threats.

OPC UA (OLE for Process Control Unified Architecture): OPC UA provides a secure communication protocol for industrial automation that delivers improved security features beyond those of previous protocols.

Patch Management: Regular updates to software and firmware help fix confirmed security vulnerabilities.

Penetration Testing: Penetration Testing involves creating a mock cyberattack to discover weak points within systems or networks.

Phishing: Social engineering attacks involve attackers tricking users into disclosing sensitive information like usernames and passwords through deceptive emails or websites.

Programmable Logic Controller (PLC): Programmable Logic Controllers (PLCs) represent specialized computers dedicated to industrial automation tasks. PLCs are often integrated into SCADA systems.

Purdue Model: The Purdue Model establishes five distinct levels of control in industrial automation systems each requiring different security measures. This is commonly used for network segmentation.

Quantum-Resistant Cryptography: Quantum computers threaten current encryption techniques which lead to the development of algorithms that resist quantum attacks.

Ransomware: This form of malware locks a victim's files through encryption and requires payment of a ransom to unlock them.

Remote Terminal Unit (RTU): A Remote Terminal Unit (RTU) works within SCADA systems to gather sensor and actuator data before sending it to the main control center.

Risk Assessment: The procedure involves pinpointing possible security risks followed by their detailed analysis and evaluation.

Risk Management: Risk management requires organizations to identify potential risks followed by their analysis and assessment and subsequently treat and monitor them.

Role-Based Access Control (RBAC): This access control method operates by assigning users to specific roles with predefined permissions to streamline access management while increasing security measures.

SCADA (Supervisory Control and Data Acquisition): SCADA systems enable the supervision and management of industrial operations which are frequently utilized in essential infrastructure.

Secure Access Service Edge (SASE): Secure Access Service Edge (SASE) offers network security functions through cloud delivery which includes secure web gateways and VPN capabilities.

Secure Shell (SSH): Secure Shell (SSH) functions as a network protocol that enables secure access and management of remote computers.

Security Information and Event Management (SIEM): This system gathers security data from multiple sources to analyze and manage information which offers organizations a complete view of their security status.

Social Engineering: Social engineering involves manipulating people to gain access to sensitive information or systems.

Stuxnet: The Stuxnet malware represents an advanced cyberattack that targeted Iranian nuclear facilities and demonstrated how digital attacks can lead to physical destruction.

Supply Chain Attack: These cyber-attacks target vendors or suppliers of organizations to compromise their systems.

Threat Intelligence: Threat intelligence comprises data about potential cybersecurity threats as well as vulnerabilities and attacker tactics techniques and procedures known as TTPs.

Virtual Private Network (VPN): The Virtual Private Network (VPN) technology forms a secure encrypted link between users and networks to protect data during remote access sessions.

Vulnerability: A system or network weakness represents an exploitable flaw that attackers can use to compromise security.

Vulnerability Management: Vulnerability Management includes the steps of locating weaknesses, evaluating their risks, and implementing corrective actions.

Zero Trust: The security model known as Zero Trust requires consistent user and device authentication before allowing access to system resources without pre-established trust.

This glossary contains a complete overview of the essential terminology used throughout the book. The provided definitions maintain brevity and readability so they can be understood by people of all backgrounds. Readers should seek further resources to gain comprehensive understanding of any of these terms.

Made in United States
Orlando, FL
04 November 2026

90207805R00079